# IT'S A
# GIRL

## Mary Keating

**outskirts
press**

*For Jim and David who inspired me,*

*And LASSIE, the dog I loved!*

"Choose the least important day in your life. It will be important enough."

Thorton Wilder, *Our Town*

"Oh, Mr. Webb, Is there any culture or love of beauty in Grover's Corners?"

Mr. Webb: "Well, there ain't much --- not in the sense you mean...

No Ma'am, there ain't much culture. But maybe...we've got a lot of pleasures of a kind here: we love the sun coming up over the mountains in the morning, we watch the birds...and we watch the change of seasons; yes, everybody knows about them. But those other things --- you're right Ma'am there ain't much."

Thorton Wilder, *Our Town*

# Table of Contents

## PART II

# Introduction

*THROUGH THE YEARS many friends and acquaintances have told me how magical and wonderful growing up in Bradford, Pennsylvania was during the 1950s and early 1960s. To those of us born in Bradford, the "High Grade Oil Metropolis of the World," it was mythical. The earth produced the Bradford Oilfield. Wildcatters bought up land that went for $1000 an acre in the 1870s. Gushers poured into the skies and over the land. The Bradford Exchange established in 1878 recorded more than one million dollars in transactions in one day that year.*

*The memory of the heyday of oil production and the first and oldest refinery in the nation, Kendall Refining Company, trickled down from the creeks to every town resident in every decade.*

*Five powerful men held the strings in Bradford in the 1950s. They were the breath of the newspaper, the radio station, and the lumber and oil producing companies. In the hills and back yards were hundreds of visible derricks pumping oil. During the oil boom there were twenty-three millionaires living on Congress Street. The street I grew up on became known as **Millionaires' Row.** As late as 1937 an oil gusher called Music Mountain, three miles south of Lewis Run, gushed forth with 44 barrels per hour. By the end of the 1940s, 292 wells were drilled leaving several oil companies very rich.*

*Names like Oil Well Supply, Pure Oil Company, Minard Run, Niagara Oil, United States Pipeline Company, The Option House (where stocks were sold) were as well-known as Hollywood movie stars' hands cast in concrete.*

*One man stood out from the beginning and that man was Lewis Emery. He owned 500 oil wells and 14,000 acres of land. His money built the mansion next door to my grandmother's home on Congress Street.*

*Here in **It's A Girl!**, I have written vignettes from birth through graduation from senior high school. Think of it as intimate conversations told over a drink in the ornate and historical atmosphere of the Option House in Bradford.*

*Reading **It's A Girl!** will bring you back to childhood and the power of memory in a famous town. Bradford's force and history are still felt years later by everyone shaped by the richest town in America.*

# PART ONE

# 3-3-3-3-3

I WAS BORN the third child, on the third day of the third month in 1948. After birth I lived at 33 Walker Avenue ---- 3-3-3-3-3.

My mother told me again and again of my threes, third day, third month, third child.

"Three is special," she said.

She caught her breath.

"Three wishes are always in the fairy tales and even the Bible."

When she mentioned the Bible I wondered what that meant because as Catholics we never saw a Bible nor did we study it. As a child I never found a Bible hidden in my mother's room. I used to walk in to look at her pretty dressing table. It was a real 1940s dressing table. Mirrors were on the front and top where she kept her comb and brush and three perfume bottles. I could smell the perfume leaking from the twisted top of the bottle. Whatever name it had, it was the smell of my mother when she dressed up for a cocktail party in the 1950s.

In my first seven years I remember many parties. Outdoor barbecue parties with cocktails and indoor parties with lots of booze. Summer, Halloween, Christmas Eve and New Year's Eve, grown-ups laughing and talking and being boisterous could be heard throughout the house. But later, probably after my brother was born, the parties stopped. Only one couple came up to the house after Christmas Eve service ended at the Presbyterian church. They were the parents of my childhood friend, 'Maginda.'

Since my little brother's birth, my mother's perfume bottles sat unused except when she went to an occasional dinner at the Roman Villa.

In the little drawers to the left and right were her pearls; a pair of expensive white ones and pairs of cheap white round popping necklaces made of plastic. When I was five or six, I discovered a bush in my grandmother's lawn with white round blooms the very size and look of my mother's everyday white plastic beads. I pulled a few blooms off their stem and in my little hands popped them, knowing that somehow this mysterious discovery of a white blossom in bloom connected me to my mother's pearls.

# HOUSES

MY MOTHER LIVED at 33 Walker Avenue during World War II. My father volunteered to serve. He was a Naval officer sent to Guam in the Pacific. He had two small sons aged one and two when he went away.

My brothers still remember the night their father walked through the front door dressed in his uniform. My mother was playing "Malaguena" on the piano. She had learned to play this complex piece of music by herself. The piano moved to our next house in January, 1950.

The new house was only five minutes away from Walker Avenue, but Congress Street was a world away from the group of children growing up on Walker Avenue.

The house on Congress at 126 was a ranch, set back from the street by a winding driveway. It sat next to my grandmother's large Victorian built in 1887.

The rich oil baron Emery had owned the mansion next to my grandmother's but upon death, his will stipulated that it be torn down. The next rich generation, the Dorns, built their own new house on the lot.

Walker Avenue was not fancy. It was full of simple two-story, plain wooden houses. My mother was fortunate enough to have an attic where she could house hired help. Thirty-three Walker Avenue was full of steps. Steps led up the house, steps led up to the second floor, steep steps led down the back to the large kitchen and steps went to the basement.

When my mother and father brought me home from the hospital to 33 Walker a nurse was with them. Her name was Mary Malone and she slept on the third floor while she took care of me and my mother the first few months after my birth.

My mother began keeping a Baby Book for me which only lasted for eighteen months. After we moved to Congress Street she stopped. She kept track of all my naps and feedings and my first word uttered ten months from birth: "Mama."

Before moving to Congress Street in 1950, my parents sat down at the dining room table and drew up the blueprints for their dream home. They began with the driveway which led to my grandparents' garage. There was a huge fireplace on the lawn that they designed as the focal point for the living room. They planned radiant heat because my father was tired of steam heat.

The kitchen was long and narrow with a bar cupboard. French doors from the dining room opened to the back yard. One bedroom and small bath next to the dining room was designated the boys' room (to share). Up five steps past the living room with built-in bookshelves were two bedrooms and a full bath. My parents did not plan for two more babies who immediately arrived. When we moved in January, 1950 in the snow and cold of Bradford my mother was pregnant with her fourth child, my younger sister.

For the rest of my mother's life she reminisced about Walker Avenue where she had spent two years alone while my father was in the Pacific. She had a few women friends like Tommy Clark, who lived next door and had the only clothes dryer on the street. Tommy let my mother come dry her clothes at her house. The families on Walker Avenue all had girls and boys who were my brothers' ages: the Kreinsons, the Pringles, the Clarks, the Donohues; Ukranian, Italian, Irish, and English were all there playing happily. When one of the children had a birthday party my mother always included me. I would sit in my high chair and smile and wave to all the children.

On Congress Street there were one or two girls up the street but no little boys. The neighbors in the area around the ranch were elderly. My grandmother and grandfather, the neighbors next door, the Boyle Seniors,

Mrs. Dorn on the other side and Mrs. Dorn's chauffeur, called Big Mike, replaced the children of Walker Avenue.

I grew up with the elderly and loved it! I had the greatest freedom to roam in all their back yards and never did they yell "get out of my yard."

I discovered every pine tree, every grate on their property, every porch and shortcut between my little world of four houses. Grates covered the two-foot holes which were built to catch the overspill of water. They were set across the hole next to the basement windows. They were built of the same strong Bradford pipe that was used to move oil. Each grate was about twelve inches from the basement window. When I was about seven I climbed under a grate at Mrs. Dorn's house. I squeezed my thin little body down the hole and sat there crouched low while my parents yelled and screamed in the ranch house.

At some point, not unlike Pooh Bear, I thought, "This might not be the best place to be, what if I can't get out? Who will find me?" It was a very safe place but scary if I couldn't get out. With that thought I squeezed my head, then shoulders, arms and hands over the top of the grate then I pulled my waist, legs, and feet up and I was free. Whew!

I continued my way across the pachysandra to a stone wall near Dorn's property. There I jumped down to the grass and tumbled and stood up knowing I was in the back lot area of Congress Street where folks kept their garages. The dusty unpaved alley led to Second Ward School. It seemed safe enough to walk down. No dogs came at me. But I was glad to reach Elm Street and turn right toward Congress Street once more. I stopped at Smith's Market and bought Fifth Avenue candy bars and pop. Then I continued up Dorn's driveway to my grandmother's flagstones alongside her house. I called the flagstones the "bumpy tracks" as they were my special place to hide.

I listened. I watched. There was no yelling coming from the ranch. It was quiet again.

I could walk in the front door and run to my bedroom to trace Winnie the Pooh characters, listen to "Bozo Under the Sea" or hug my stuffed Lassie dog.

# BRADFORD LEGACY

BRADFORD FIRST BECAME famous worldwide after oil was discovered in Titusville in August 1859. The "black gold" shot up from the earth in Bradford beginning in 1871. After oil was discovered "rigs multiplied like rabbits in Australia." By 1880 Bradford produced 20,138,091 barrels per year! Bradford's nickname became "High Grade Oil Metropolis of the World."

As the decades went by oil kept making millionaires out of the industrious and lucky men in town. If you were born in Bradford the memory of Bradford producing oil grabbed hold like a cell in your brain. Wealth and power were something in the air; in the smell from the Kendall Refinery; in the Tuna Creek (crick) in the hills, in the deep dark earth, or in the derricks pumping in the back yards.

Rich surrounded you! To be the richest town in America and to produce 70 % of the world's high grade oil and to have the largest Oil Exchange in the world was damn rich!! Bradford's reputation echoed all over the world!

In the 1950s rich and middle class and poor were palpable equations. Bradford embraced its image for one last decade in the 1950s before its own threads began to tear apart. Oil began to be drilled in Texas and most of the producers began to follow it there. Bradford land was not offering up its precious black gold in the same quantities. The earth was tired.

All the Dorn sons followed the oil to Texas. One brick building on Main Street with Forest Oil etched in the glass window remained.

Mrs. Dorn's grandchildren arrived from Texas every summer in the 1950s with their parents, dogs and luggage. They were all going to the family estate: Glendorn.

In early June I would see Big Mike drive the custom-built Cadillac filled with twenty-six grandchildren down the driveway and head out of town to Glendorn. The Cadillac was baby blue and twice as long as any regular Cadillac.

Glendorn was part of the mythology and story of growing up in Bradford. It stirred every child's imagination and if one were lucky to be invited there then Christmas had arrived early!

Christmas did arrive early one summer morning when my mother answered the phone. It was a call from Mrs. Dorn inviting my younger sister and me to Glendorn. We were told to bring our swimsuits and we would be returned by 5 p.m. We were picked up in the Rolls Royce. Big Mike left the driveway with my sister and me in the back seat. He drove down West Corydon for what felt like miles. I didn't know where I was.

Big Mike turned right on Glendorn Drive and came to a wrought iron gate and a box with red and black buttons. He pressed the black button and the gate opened. He drove through beautiful forests of pine and hemlock and maple and oak with small lakes dotting the landscape. When we reached the 'Big' house he let us out to spend the day anyway we wanted.

Glendorn had all the leisure activities of the day: horses and tennis and hiking and skeet-shooting and swimming and a huge café building where kids could sit at drugstore stools and order a sundae for free.

I walked into the dressing room and a heavenly smell filled my nose. It smelled like pine or something natural. There were so many big white puffy towels I thought I was in a hotel.

My little sister and I walked out to the pool and jumped in. The water was clean and a turquoise color. Beneath the water in the deep end was a wrought iron tea table and two chairs. We dove down and tried to sit in the chairs and pretend to have a tea party.

We swam like ducks splashing and playing in the pool with these total strangers, the Dorn grandchildren. We heard a few of the names: Brooks, Leslie, John, Tucker, Daley. None of the Dorns said hello as they had no idea who we were.

Our day was a gift from their grandmother, Mrs. Dorn, because she was a good friend of my grandmother.

After our swim my little sister and I sat in the café and ate a sundae.

As a child there were so many sensations with no words. A day at Glendorn lived in a sensory place that could not be duplicted. It was magical!

Mrs. Dorn extended her invitation to my mother for about four years. Then it stopped, when I was probably twelve, and life was turning into new and different choices.

# PATERNAL GRANDFATHER

MY GRANDFATHER WAS born in Broadford, County Limerick, Ireland in 1893. He died 77 years later in Bradford. He was the eldest of four children so he was chosen to leave Ireland and come to America to find a job and send money home. His parents, John and Catherine Creagh Keating, were tenant farmers who survived the Great Famine!

My grandfather tried the oil fields of Texas first, then moved to Boston, where he worked on the city trolley. When he heard through the grapevine of other Irish in the Bradford, Pennsylvania area he left Boston. The sound of the word Bradford reminded him so much of his own village in Broadford, County Limerick, Ireland that he settled down. He bought 75 acres for his dairy farm. Sadly, he sold his land after World War II when small houses were being built and sold to veterans; land was precious. Before moving he named three streets: Keating, Prendergast, (my grand-mother's maiden name) and Constitution.

As a child I thought he was a very handsome man. I found a photograph of him dressed in his "Sunday best." I believe it was taken in America. He spent his money that day.

Unfortunately, I only knew him eight years before some rift between my father and grandfather stopped all his visits to our home. I never forgot him and to this day he still haunts my dreams.

# PATERNAL GRANDMOTHER

WHEN MY GRANDMOTHER arrived at Ellis Island, the immigration officer told her to change her name. She was Bridget Prendergast of County Mayo and he would not accept that name. Bridget was a ridiculed name. It was cheap and Irish and it implied her being anything from a prostitute to just a lowly domestic servant. My grandmother was twenty and that was her first impression of America. They hated her name.

My young, sweet, frightened grandmother became Bertha Gertrude at Ellis Island. From that day forward she had to accept the Americanization of her own name.

She worked as a domestic servant for a rich oil family in Bradford for three years until she met my grandfather.

I never knew her. But I have seen one photograph of her in her "Sunday best."

I like to think my grandparents had their pictures taken on the same day. It might have been my grandfather's way of courting Bridget. I will never know.

Bridget/Bertha had a horrific time with breast cancer and died of it at the young age of forty-eight. Before she died, she birthed my father, Edward Creagh Keating, in 1921 at the Bradford Hospital.

# MY MOTHER

MY MOTHER WAS sent to a boarding school, Shipley, near Philadelphia, away from her friends, who all went to Bradford High School. She wrote my grandmother letters every night when she was sixteen and poured her heart out. She tried to get good grades, which she did, straight 'A's but she still had to stay for four years.

My mother wanted to come home. Now and again while watching my mother I would catch a sadness that I could not understand. Now and again when she spoke there was a catch in her words and she seemed to me the saddest person I ever met. But we never talked about anything. She would drift off in a daze, distracted, suffering from something no little child could understand. She often looked at me like she didn't understand what a little girl meant after two boys. I kept up my side of the unspoken bargain and tried to be as good as I could be. But I wasn't always able to keep her calm. And when she got angry at me, I had to defend my little self by screaming back at her.

I knew my mother had been given a 1939 Packard convertible when she came home from Shipley. She showed me the photo. My God so pretty! There she was: young, attractive, extremely smart, and rich (my grandparents had money). She met a boy from town who was poor and Irish, quiet and honest, when a chum set them up on a date. My mother was happy to be with a young man from Bradford. He loved to talk with my mother. He loved her laugh.

There was a season of dating when she strolled with him beneath the lampposts of town and then danced at the Gold Room at the Emery Hotel. She drove the young man and her chums around in her Packard.

But she still had to go to college at William and Mary in Williamsburg, Virginia and he was off to St Bonaventure in Allegany, New York. It would be four long years before they could marry, she had told him.

They began to write love letters to each other. My father disappeared into the library for hours writing his first letters. He censored his own passions because he never knew who might intercept them.

After two years of courtship and many letters from my father, my mother realized she was sick of college. One year at William and Mary and she decided to quit and marry this handsome Irish boy who helped his dad with the dairy farm. They flashed upon each other like lightning. They were married in the St. Bernard rectory because my mother was not Catholic. She was not allowed to wed in the church.

Twenty-two years after they married, pregnant with her fifth child, there was a moment I remember when my mother laid down on the couch in the living room with her yellow house dress on.

I was five and looked at her all ballooned up. She asked me "what do you want Mary, a baby boy or a baby girl?" I stood there feeling little next to this whale on the couch and looked at the glasses framing her pretty face and wavy brown hair and brown eyes and answered,

"A boy."

She smiled at me. She gave birth to a boy.

And that is when the money rows started. My mother kept a clean house with five children underfoot. She prepared meals as best she could but sometimes they just didn't go over with my father.

The night of tomato vegetable soup still stands out in my mind: baby J in a highchair, the two older brothers across the table, my sister next to my mother and me to the right of my father. We all dipped our spoons into the tomato vegetable soup.

There was a silence that sent shivers up my back. I could feel my father's deep dark psyche. He loved my mother but there were times he could not control invisible currents that burst open like a wound. This was one of those times.

"What is this garbage?"

"Tomato vegetable soup. It's healthy."

"Healthy? It tastes awful. Canned crap."

"Well, the children are eating it."

I was about to throw up. He pushed back his chair and dumped the soup in the kitchen sink. My brother pushed back his chair. I saw my father going for my mother at the other end of the table. My oldest brother, who was 14, jumped on the back of my father to slow him down and keep him from trying to kill my mother.

Baby J in the high chair cried. My mother sat stoically, as my father raised his fist to hit her. My father threw my brother off his back.

He turned at the last moment and grabbed his jacket in the front hall and slammed the door as he left the house. He went to a bar and drank his dinner.

My mother shook her head. We were silent as the grave but for the baby crying.

"I am not going to put up with this. Not another day," she said.

# RIPPLES

SOMEWHERE ON THE vacation page of my Baby Book there is a note about July, 1949. It says I rode the bus with Shirley Ripple to Shirley's house. I was sixteen months old.

To understand this adventure is to first think about who the Ripples were to me. My mother had hired Shirley to babysit for my two older brothers. When Shirley arrived at the front door of the ranch house my mother noticed she had a homemade dress on.

My mother, though she may not have said anything at that moment, could not put this fact away for the rest of her life. She told me the story over and over. "She had on a home-made dress that day." She never said whether that was a good thing or a bad thing in her judgment.

I had to guess if this was a good quality in a babysitter or not. It left me puzzled. I had no idea what homemade meant since all my clothes were store bought and expensive.

She did hire her, dress and all and it was the best thing my mother did in the 1950s. She gained a babysitter but more than that she gained a foster home for her daughter – me.

I was held by Shirley, at age sixteen months, on the bus on my way outside town to a small village called Degolia. The Ripples lived in a house they rented that sat perched up on a hill with long descending steps to the mailbox near the country road. Shirley had a mother and my "baby talk" turned her name into Mama Tia. Rip, her father was just that – Rip (whose real name was Frank).

Rip worked the oil fields for a rich oil producer. The fields he checked over spread up above his house and over and beyond twenty miles. The oil derricks and pipelines crisscrossed the hills and you could often hear the pumps going night and day. Sometimes he took me in his truck while he drove all over the bumpy hills and checked the oil derricks and pipe lines. I just remember being jostled up and down hills and back roads and seeing a kind man smiling at me. The smell of the fields and oil penetrated my very soul. Rip's work clothes were always blotched with oil splatters. Dark black oil soaked over his green cotton pants and shirts.

I spent a month with total strangers while my mother went to Chautauqua Lake with my father and my two older brothers.

After that first trip my mother thought to herself, "well that will work." She made an arrangement with the Ripples for me to spend more months in the summer and fall and spring. I never knew when I would be shipped out of town and I never heard a reason for my going. My brothers never spent a night there.

There were five bedrooms at this unexplained foster home. My room seemed big to me. The others were filled with their daughter M, who was a teen-ager, Grandma, Mama Tia and Rip. The fifth was a small sewing room. By this time Shirley was off to business school. I occupied her bedroom.

Their house was homey with white curtains, area rugs, a large kitchen, dining room and parlor. There was a piano in the parlor that Mama Tia played each week before she went to a small church down the country road. There she played the piano and sang with the choir.

Rip rose at 4:30 a.m. and went downstairs to dress in his little room off the kitchen. He sat in a rocker in the kitchen when he came home from work. A deer skin hung over the slats of the rocker. The washing machine was situated in an oblong room off the kitchen and there was no dishwasher or dryer. Clothes were hung outside on a big clothesline constructed of Bradford pipe.

Whenever I arrived, Mama Tia would hug me and say goodbye to my father or mother, whoever had dropped me off. I went outside immediately and played in the creek beside their house.

At nighttime after a delicious meal of goulash, made by Mama Tia, we would all converge in the living room and watch a TV program. The TV had been on all day while Grandma watched the daytime soaps: A Guiding Light, Edge of Night and As the World Turns.

I loved the evenings in the living room. I could lie down on the couch with my head in Mama Tia's lap and drift away from whatever dark thoughts I had about being dropped off with strangers. The years went by from toddler to age twelve and I was still spending long chunks of unexplained time with the Ripples.

Once in a great while my sister would be sent there with me. We shared the large bed. I drew a line down the center of it and told her to "stay on your own side." She kept on her side and I kept on mine, each of us hearing the unspoken insult of being sent away to strangers. In that darkness could be heard a train WHrrr ING and WHIS---tLing LING through the countryside.

There was no bathroom and no heat upstairs at Ripples, it was probably fifty degrees there in the winter. I had to relieve myself in an antique chamber pot. The radiant heat from my parent's's ranch house was far, far away.

On many occasions on an ordinary day I watched exhaust fumes blow upward from the Plymouth in the old wooden garage. Mama Tia tied a scarf around her head and climbed in. We were going to Singer's Country Store for household items and I was allowed to get some penny candy. I loved Singer's Country Store, its wooden floors and smells and big barrel of pickles. I picked out my root beer and licorice candy and took my little brown bag back to the front seat of the Plymouth.

On a special night, after Rip had finished smoking his pipe in the rocker in the kitchen, he would get up and make his own recipe for peanut butter fudge. He brought the hot delicious pieces of peanut butter fudge into the living room for all of us. I began to add pounds to my body during those years which prompted my older brother to call me "tubby" when I returned home.

But somehow it didn't matter. The Ripples never called me names and they took me in as one of their own daughters. They were a kind, kind family who gave me love. They never asked my mother deep personal questions as to why I was visiting them. My parents' behavior was never talked about. The mystery remained throughout my growing-up years. I only knew the Ripples wanted to officially adopt me. The word *adopt* rang of sadness in my little girl's heart! Until I was twelve, there was always the deep, unspoken, threat that someday I might be given away to the Ripples.

My mother never discussed my trips to the Ripples and I was glad. Not talking about it only added to the numerous conversations she never had with me. It helped preserve the pretense of our lives in the little ranch house.

We had deep hidden rules of silence. But sometimes the anger would break out when I got home and my mother would wash my mouth out with soap. I finally gave up trying to figure out what she did or why. Instead I kept my mouth closed and escaped into my own deep silence.

# THE ORCHID

WHEN I WAS four years old my mother gave me a birthday party. I was dressed in a beautiful blue jumper with a pretty white blouse underneath. There were balloons all around the dining room and my mother looked pretty moving in and out of the kitchen. She brought all the little four-year-old children their cake and ice cream. We played "Pin the Tail on the Donkey" and other games before we ate. We were happy running and jumping around.

My mother was happy. I blew out the candles with my little breath of air. Everyone sang *"Happy Birthday to you, Happy Birthday, dear Mary, Happy Birthday to you,"* on a cold, but sunny March afternoon.

I know I opened presents, but because of the trauma after eating my cake, I don't remember them.

One of my mother's friends stopped by to give me her gift. Neidra was blond and lovely like a movie star. She was the wife of my mother's obstetrician. They were now friends and my mother liked new friends.

Neidra came up to me with a large plastic box in her hands. Inside the plastic box was this huge, strange looking petal thing. It was not a flower I had ever seen in my four years. It frightened me.

When Neidra took it out of the box and tried to pin it on my little body over my blue jumper I began to cry.

I did not want the orchid which I had no name for. It frightened me but my mother did not care.

"No, mommy." I tried to tear it off.

My mother was so embarrassed by my

behavior she immediately sent me out of the room to the cellar steps.

I sat on the cellar steps and cried. All my little friends went home. Neidra went home. I sat on the steps and cried some more. I tore off the orchid and threw it down the cellar stairs.

It was the last birthday party my mother ever gave me for the rest of my life.

# ART CLASSES

WHEN I WAS eleven my mother found a woman in town who gave art lessons in her basement. I was taken at night to West Corydon Street for my first lessons in oil painting.

The dark frightened me. I was down in a little basement with a few adults and one young boy named Jay.

I had my own easel, canvas, oil paints, and brushes and I was fascinated.

I did everything Mrs. George told me to do. I sketched and mixed colors and painted her cattails and her vases and her apples in still lifes for weeks and weeks. When I took them home my mother hung them up in the hallway. I was quite pleased in a quiet way that my mother thought enough to hang them up. No one in my family said a word about my paintings.

In the final sessions Mrs. George told the five of us to bring something from home we would like to paint. She would let us paint freely.

I took my Raggedy Ann and Raggedy Andy dolls with me. I set them up in the corner of the basement and sat right by them and began to paint something I loved.

They turned out so fine and vivid. I gave them a green background and sat them on a few books to ground them in space. They were so sweet with their black-button eyes, little smiles, and red hair.

I loved the painting. My mother loved it too. She kept it the rest of her life and always had it sitting somewhere in the house so others could see what her daughter had painted.

# GOD

WHEN FIRST GRADE arrived I was taken to Catholic religious education classes at St. Bernard's elementary school, where tall women in black habits filled the hallways. I was given my first catechism with a blue cover and thus began my first introduction to God. Before the classes I had noticed my father went somewhere on Sundays with my brothers, and it was called Mass. I climbed my secret and favorite "umbrella tree" (my name for it) and looked at the sky while they were gone.

From the beginning *God made me and God loves me* on the first page of my catechism I was hooked and haunted by a presence I had only found in my umbrella tree. The first time

I went to Mass with my father, the statues sent me into a heavenly reverie that lasted a lifetime. When I saw the large statue of the Pieta in St Bernard's I knew I would run away after church and weep at its beauty.

Thus began my thread of Catholic childhood teachings, Mass, and climbing the umbrella tree to see further than my home inside. The sky offered me the same haunting mystery that the church did in a holy, spiritual way.

I was preparing for my First Communion that year of discovery. The answers to the catechism questions seemed like fun to me. They came easily and I was fascinated by this tall woman with a black habit standing in front of the room. Her rosary tied around her waist also got my attention. I was being lifted up by this faith that my father gave me.

My mother rarely went to church or Mass. She was not Catholic or of any religion that I could see. Her mother, my grandmother, attended the Presbyterian church in town. We never went near it. My mother had agreed to raise her children Catholic and she never said a word otherwise.

By First Communion day I was thrilled. I would be receiving the body and blood of our Lord in the Holy Eucharist. Not that I knew what it was only that I trusted the tall nun who had taught me that "God loves me."

I was taken to the children's clothing store with my mother to pick out a new communion dress.

The saleswoman was ready with several dresses for the First Communion ceremonies. I was happy with the dress my mother chose. It was white, lacey, and lovely.

The big day came and there I was at the alter kneeling and waiting for the priest to come to me. There he was with that gold chalice. I breathed a happy excited breath and opened my mouth like a baby bird. He placed the wafer on my tongue. Christ was there! Now I was in heaven with him.

Afterwards, when we had all reached our

pews again, the choir sang "Ave Maria" and I bit my lip so I wouldn't cry.

It was my first Mass in the Catholic Church and all I knew was a key to something had been given me that morning. I was not in the ranch house. I was not at Ripples or in their church sitting like a stranger. I was in this magnificent church with its stained-glass windows and statues and the beautiful Pieta and God.

After Mass all the families who knew each other, including the Yates with little Martha, walked in the May sunshine to the Emery Hotel.

The Emery Hotel was owned by the Emery family. Grace Emery built it with her family's oil money in 1929 and dedicated it to her late father, Lewis Emery. It was seven stories high and built with local Hanley brick. Inside, on the first floor, was the Gold Room which was the crème de la crème restaurant in town. It was so special to be going there for my communion breakfast, not the local diner or the Howard Johnson's nearby.

My parents ordered breakfast and drank Bloody Marys for themselves. The adults talked and drank. The little girls sat happily guarding their gloves next to them and the big pink linen napkin unfolded on their laps. We could see our little white shoes and we could snap open and shut our little white purses. I opened mine and saw the lovely cotton hanky my grandmother had given me for this special First Communion.

# PETER PAN

IN 1954 PETER Pan was going to be broadcast on television from Broadway with Mary Martin as Peter Pan. I was six.

Our television set was not installed so E, my childhood friend, asked me to come see it at her house, two houses up the street.

We spent the afternoon outside at our tea party. A little girl's dream come true. E had a play tea set with cups and saucers and a small table and two chairs for the two of us. There was even a pretty creamer and sugar bowl. Jeanette, E's housekeeper (and second mother to E), brought real tea out to us. I brought chocolate chip cookies my mother baked for the tea party.

Jeanette always wore a white uniform which made me think she might be a nurse. And if she wasn't a nurse then she was the kindest woman on the street, like an angel. She always took good care of E; she loved E like her own child.

Two sweet little girls drenched in pink and gold sunlight streaming down to the sidewalk and their young heads in 1954.

E blew softly on her tea.

"Hot."

"Yep."

"Does your Mama work?"

"Nah, she is home with us."

"I like your Mama's chocolate chip cookies. My Mama's never home."

"Where is she?"

"I think she plays bridge. And stuff. Jeanette does all the work all day."

We both took a sip of tea together and smiled at each other. We had a friend.

"I want you to come to my house and watch Peter Pan."

"Is it okay with your Mama?"

"Jeanette will be with us, I told ya' my Mama's not home."

At 5:15 p.m. my father drove the Studebaker up the driveway and entered the house. He leaned over my mother who was lying in the couch and asked, "How was your day?"

"Oh, fine," said my mother.

Peter Pan was on at 7 p.m. and I wondered if my mother could get my father fed and get me out the door.

"I have a meeting tonight. So I have to eat earlier," said my father.

"Go wash up, Mary. We're having dinner earlier."

"Mommy, E asked me over for Peter Pan tonight. May I go?"

"What time?"

"Seven."

"We can manage. You get your pajamas on and walk over after dinner."

I was thrilled.

"Your father will pick you up at 9:30 and walk you home."

"Yes, Mommy."

Dinner went quickly and there were no rows. My father used the bathroom first; then I went in and brushed my teeth and put on my pajamas. I was so happy it was working out.

My father drove off to his meeting and I walked down the driveway and two houses up the street. I saw my father watching that I made it inside E's house. Jeanette opened the door.

She led me into the fancy living room where the TV sat on a bureau in the corner.

E and I sat twenty inches from the screen. E got a blanket and put it over both of us. We cuddled together and then it started.

There it was right in E's living room: the Darling home in England on the screen. And there was Peter Pan flying into the Darling's living room window looking for his lost shadow.

And thus began our journey to Never, Never Land.

# CREEK or CRICK

BRADFORD WAS CRISSCROSSED and circled by creeks, beautiful creeks that gurgled all the time. The biggest creek was Tunungwant (an Indian name) shortened to "Tuna Crick." "Crick" was how it was pronounced by those born in Bradford. Tuna Creek looked like a river to a child especially in the spring after all the snows melted.

I was born after the big flood when several streets by Tuna Creek flooded and houses were lost near Davis and Amm streets.

I never grew up thinking of a flood coming. Flood control came in and built walls to keep the creeks back from the streets.

One of my favorite creeks was at Ripples. It

ran down the hills, passed alongside Ripples' garage, sank underneath the road to appear a few miles further in someone else's back yard near Custer City Drive-In.

I spent hours dipping my little hands and feet in the cool, clear water that could make you feel you were newly born. I often picked up a rock and much to my delight I found a crayfish underneath. Not liking the disturbance he swam backwards, which I found fascinating to watch. SWSSH his tail moved and backwards he swam under another rock and into the sediment. He completely disappeared from view and I was left wondering, "where is he?"

# BACK YARDS

ALL THROUGH CHILDHOOD I roamed the neighbors' back yards and climbed up the stone stairs behind Dorn's huge house next door.

I climbed to the third tier of their back yard and looked out at the world with its big sky and hills. One day I discovered a driveway entrance from South Avenue, the next street up, used for deliveries to the garden. The garden was a long and wide piece of earth taken care of by Dorn's gardener, Joe. He often was there digging up carrots. He waved to me. I ran over to him. My young mind knew he was kind.

"Here," he said.

He handed me a freshly pulled carrot. I bit into it right away. It was delicious.

"I'm goin' to take yer grandma her favorite tomatoes today."

I smiled. My blue eyes looked down at the orange carrots with their green leafy tops. It was the biggest garden in the world to me.

When I climbed back down the tiers of steps from visiting Joe, I could see Dorn's kitchen windows. Betty, their German cook, called to me from inside the kitchen. I walked in the side door and turned left to the spacious kitchen.

She had just finished baking oatmeal raisin cookies.

"Here you are, sweetheart."

She handed me warm cookies and poured a tall glass of milk.

I sat at the big farm table. I looked at the pretty Spanish tiles all over the walls.

"Yumm."

Betty smiled at me.

I finished in silence and pure sensory delight. When I stood up Betty took my hand and walked me to the door. I left as quietly as I had entered. I knew that it was special to be in this big rich kitchen knowing Mrs. Dorn sat somewhere in another section of the house.

Mrs. Dorn had a caretaker as she had trouble walking. I knew my grandmother and Mrs. Dorn were friends and that they played bridge together and drank something called a Martini.

I got back to my yard and went to my umbrella tree. I broke off a small twig and made a slingshot out of it with a big rubber band I had found in my grandmother's sewing kit.

I was thrilled to play alone in my little world. Whoever seemed to be protecting me was my best friend. And I sensed, at age five, that someone was looking out for me when I was outdoors in the grass and lilacs and hollyhocks and fish ponds and pine trees and pansies of three back yards.

# THE SMALL BEDROOM

I HAD THE small room in the house. It measured just long enough to set a twin bed with a spindle frame snug against the wall toward the picture window. My father built a wall partition with a heavy, ugly, gray rubber door that slid to the left and right.

The room on the other side of the partition, which was at least 12x12 feet, was given to my younger sister. I had to walk through her room to get to my bedroom every morning and night and to make a bathroom visit. I learned to tiptoe to avoid waking her; I learned where all the squeaks were in the floorboards under the carpet.

Inside my room was the wonderland I created. I had Zippy the chimpanzee, Bozo the clown, records of "Under the Sea" with Bozo, a life-sized Lassie, several 45 rpm phonograph records of cowboys singing, life-size bird kits I painted and put together, books I loved like *Winnie the Pooh* and a desk with a window showing the curved driveway.

I spent many hours looking down the driveway when I was tracing my *Winnie the Pooh* characters on wax paper.

The driveway had a stone wall that often was bumped as we all learned to drive backwards when we reached our learners' permit age. My mother was famous for saying to anyone "the architect must have been drunk when he designed that driveway."

In 1958 my father put up the biggest backboard and basketball hoop in town. I could see it from my window. The pipes holding the wooden backboard were strong Bradford pipes dug two feet deep into the earth to brace it. Nothing moved that backboard, not boys or cars or basketballs or rain or sleet or snow piled six feet up against it in the winters.

Since my older brother played basketball in high school his friends were the first to arrive. But after he graduated and went off to Annapolis the younger boys who loved basketball came to play in the spring. They arrived after dinner and played 'til dark. My father decided they needed a light. He put up a huge spotlight that lit up the driveway and several yards nearby. It shone into my little bedroom until they went home, usually around 10 p.m.

I immediately found that I could not sit and trace *Winnie the Pooh* characters any longer. I wanted to play basketball. I joined the boys. And they let me. I began to play every night in the spring and summer. My best shot was from the laundry room door to the net. It was a long shot and I could "SWISH" it every time. Today, it would be called a "3-pointer."

One night, a player named Donny (who was the star player on the high school team) walked up the driveway. I nearly fainted! I developed a schoolgirl crush on him. He had dishwater blond hair and a beautiful lanky body. But even more important, he saw that I could play well and shoot amazingly well so he started to pick me for his team. I was in heaven. Donny wanted me on his team! I understood that this was not romance. It was admiration. We were basketball buddies. My esteem grew with all the other guys.

So every night after dinner, for five years in the spring and summer, the thump, thump, thump resounded throughout the neighborhood. None of the neighbors living near the driveway court complained of the Thump! Thump! Thump! Happy boys and one very happy girl playing her favorite game of basketball. It was a time that none of the boys ever forgot.

Later, in ninth grade, I traveled with Donny's father and Donny's girlfriend, Martha, to all of the out-of -town games. His father drove us up and down the hills in the fall and winter to all the small towns of Pennsylvania just to see Donny play.

Donny graduated from high school and I

never saw him again. My father tore down the backboard and hoop when he sold the house seven years after I graduated from senior high school. It was a sad moment. I never played basketball again with boys.

# SECOND WARD SCHOOL

WHEN I LET go of my mother's hand to enter Second Ward School at age six I heard a cry in my throat that I kept buried. It was the longest walk of my life down Congress Street knowing I did not want to leave my mother.

Around Christmas the teacher asked my mother if I would draw the Virgin Mary for the manger scene. My mother said yes. I spread big brown drawing paper on the dining room floor and opened several jars of acrylic paint.

I sketched the Virgin Mary's outline and was amazed that the pictures from my catechism helped me draw her form right there on the paper on the tiled linoleum floor. I had no idea I could draw. I remember thinking, no one is yelling at me about spilling paint on the floor. My father and siblings seemed to walk gingerly by during the two days it took me to finish the painting.

After it dried, my mother rolled it up carefully. We put our winter coats and mittens and hats and boots on and slushed through the snow and cold (Bradford often had the coldest temperatures in the nation in the winter) to arrive at the school. I handed over the painting of the Blessed Virgin Mary which was ninety per cent blue paint. The teacher stapled it on the board for the first-grade Christmas manger mural.

My father did not take a picture of me with his camera. No one took a picture of the mural in the school. It was taken down by the janitor over the Christmas break and probably tossed in the garbage. I never saw my painting of the Virgin Mary again.

# REXY ROGERS

THEY MOVED INTO the town with an oil company. Mr. Doug Rogers, his wife, Betty, Patricia, the younger sister and Rex. They rented a big Victorian at the corner of Kane and Congress Street. My mother took immediately to Betty who wore her hair up in a bun and was a good bridge player. They weren't here long but the time they were was never forgotten.

Rex had light brown hair and blue eyes and the sweetest smile I had ever seen. He was slight in build. I towered over him in second grade. When he walked up Congress Street on his way home, I hid up on the stone wall by my grandmother's house and waited like a spider: little second-grader ready to pounce on top of him. I have no recollection of our time in second grade in our little chairs. I only know I wanted to jump on him when he passed by my house.

He fell to the ground when my seven-year-old body flew through the air and landed on top of him. He cried for his Mother.

"Mommy Mommy."

I got up and teased him.

He ran up the street. Later, on a Saturday afternoon, he invited me to his home for cookies. We ended up in the abandoned field behind his big house. Among the weeds and overgrown grass he pulled down his pants and showed me his little penis. His eyes fluttered down his body. He wanted my dress up around my waist. I stopped and wouldn't do more.

Rexy waited. He looked at my belly button.

He looked at me.

*Those eyes are going to get a lot of girls to do what he wants.*

He was trembling. I was curious to see his whole visual form. My brothers never showed me their bodies.

It began to rain. We stopped looking at each other's anatomy (he did not see below my belly button) and went inside the house for more cookies. I ran home and told no one. That was my first and last Saturday in the abandoned field behind Rexy's house. We kept to open back yards and played Cinderella with other little girls on the street, always keeping most of our clothes on.

Later in the year my second-grade teacher, Miss McKitrick, called my parents and told them someone must come in for a conference about my behavior. My parents had no idea what she was talking about. My father walked down Congress Street with me. We sat with Miss McKitrick in the classroom. She looked at my father.

"Mary must be disciplined. I hear she is jumping off your wall on top of Rex Rogers."

My father looked stunned. Silence seeped under the little maple desk where I sat.

He looked at me. He looked at Miss McKitrick.

Miss McKitrick looked at him.

"I hope you will speak to her about manners."

"She'll do better."

My father didn't want to sit any longer on those little chairs so he got up. The conference was over.

We walked outside in the cool late afternoon.

He turned to me and said, "You like Rex don't you?"

Now that was a shock.

I nodded, yes.

"I don't want you to jump on him anymore."

I nodded again and that was the end of it. No punishment.

The Rogers left town as quickly as they arrived. Twelve years later, when I was eighteen, I saw Rex in Texas and he took me out to dinner at a beautiful restaurant with bayou themes. What was strange is the feeling we seemed to have between us. Neither of us could speak of our feelings for each other but he knew he was attracted to me and I knew I was attracted to him. I don't know why it did not go further but we were just visiting for the night and I would be gone in the morning with my family, headed for Biloxi, Mississippi. He drove me back to the hotel in his red MG convertible. He gave me a wonderful, sensuous kiss goodnight. I knew he was "rich" now. I had no idea of "rich" when Rexy showed me his little boy privates.

# VORTEX

OUTSIDE WAS ALWAYS pulling me. The best spot in the whole area of back yards between our ranch house and my grandmother's Victorian was across from the garbage shed. Mud gathered in the spring. Often clean sheets and towels were hanging the length of my grandmother's porch. The porch was all wood with walls painted white. I loved to see the sheets flapping in the southwestern wind. From the porch I could see the hills of home filled with trees reaching toward the sky.

Across from the porch was the vortex where my father built my swing set. I must have been six or seven. He must have had some oil men help him because it was made out of solid Bradford pipe, the same pipe used for drilling oil. The swing set was solid as the hills. Climbing on the large wooden seats with E next to me took us up, up, up! The thrill of no feet on the muddy ground in spring never left me. I could see into the clouds and blue sky.

The other little girl who played in my vortex of earth was 'Maginda.' She moved to Congress Street when I was seven and a half. We became friends instantly when her father brought her to our back yard. We only lived five houses away from each other. Her father was married to his second wife, Maginda's step-mother. Whenever I visited Maginda her step-mother was verbally abusing her. We bonded, seeing similarities in our mothers. The same bond E and I had felt about our mothers at our young age of four.

One day while it was spring and muddy in the vortex I got the idea of cutting Maginda's finger so we could become blood sisters. I'm not really sure where the idea came from, but as a child I liked to imagine it came from the Senecas I often saw in Salamanca. I had a small pocket knife from Rip which was shiny and had a brown handle.

I took my hand and cut my finger. A small amount of blood poured out. I took Maginda's hand all soft and pink and cut her index finger. She cried out a little. We put the blood together finger to finger, like ET, and that was it.

"We are blood sisters, forever," I told Maginda.

Across from the swings was the garbage shed for my grandmother's house. It was about ten feet tall. We got up on the top by piling chairs up and helping each other scoot upward. Then we flew off and landed in the mud. I am not sure why neither of us ever broke a bone jumping like that.

At night I began to dream of flying off the top of my grandmother's house which was sixty-five feet tall. It towered over all the other houses in the neighborhood. I could feel my dream body fly in my nightgown above the arborvitae trees, above the driveway, far away over the back yards of Congress Street into oblivion and the stars.

# MENAGERIE

WE HAD WHITE ducks, a rabbit, a mutt, a Newfoundland named Pepper, and a bunny. I wasn't sure how we got to have all these animals, but somehow they all arrived in our back yard within the city limits.

The ducks were fun to feed. Each night after dinner I would go outside with Sugar Corn Pops and throw them to the quacking happy creatures. When my mother decided they were too big, Big Mike offered to take them to Glendorn. I thought, *how lucky these ducks are to live the rest of their lives in Glendorn.* I got to ride out to Glendorn one fall day with Big Mike and watch him release the ducks into the large pond. They splashed around and within an instant knew they were home.

No more Sugar Corn Pops from a little girl in a back yard.

Pepper was discovered by my mother while riding through the country back roads. She spotted a rough and tumble wooden house in the hills with a tire swing hanging from a tree and she stopped. They had Newfoundland puppies. She bought one. No thought of the size at all. Clueless. When it grew to be big enough for me to ride I climbed on its back. We paraded around the back yard: me and my large dog-pony. One afternoon she announced she was giving Pepper away. My mother finally could see it was too big for the yard and since no dog was allowed inside the house it really had no protection.

The mutt arrived one day when a farm boy my mother found came to the back yard with his arms full of mutts, looking like mixed Collies. Our back-yard fish pond was empty of fish so he put them in there. My little sister picked out one and I picked out another. My puppy was running and jumping around the circular pond. I named him Frisky on the spot. My mother decided the docile one my sister liked would be better. I saw Frisky go in an instant. My little sister's mutt was named Tippy for the white tip on her tail. She was not allowed to enter the house so my father built a run in the driveway, then he emptied out an old icebox for Tippy to sleep in. I was horrified to see Tippy all curled up in such a small space outdoors.

One day Tippy ran to the end of her run and the postman panicked and kicked her. She was never the same after that. My sister never scooped poop or played with her or fed her all the years we watched her grow. My father took care of Tippy. After the mailman incident, Tippy's personality changed so my father took Tippy one town over where my grandfather lived on a small plot of land with chickens. Tippy was happier there with my grandfather in her final days.

The bunny lived in the top compartment of the old icebox above Tippy. I had found a tiny baby bunny drowning in my grandmother's fishpond, filled with large goldfish. I gathered it from the water and nursed it back to life. I was allowed to keep it in the icebox as long as I fed it. My father seemed so kind to me at moments like this when he looked at me and said, "yes" I could keep it as a pet. I knew he didn't say much but he always seemed to be there whenever I needed something.

I fed the bunny pellets and let it out to hop in the grass, then I picked it up and put it back in the icebox. It was tame. I was around seven or eight.

In the spring, after my parents returned from a three-day outing, I had news for my father: the bunny didn't look well while they were away.

I showed my father its lifelessness. He took one look at the bunny and then he looked at me and told me "get in the car."

He put the sick bunny on my lap and closed the door. He got in the driver's seat and drove across town and then a few more miles out of town to the veterinarian. He parked the car. I felt a tear on my cheeks, something awful was about to happen. I could feel it.

My father opened the door for me.

"He's gone," I whispered.

The bunny had taken one last gasp on my lap as my father circled the car. I could feel the stiffness. My father helped me out. We walked into the veterinarian's office and after that I don't remember much. I only remember the stench inside the building that made me nauseous.

I was quiet during the car ride home and so was my father. It was the first time I experienced death. I was sad. Very sad.

The dog my mother loved the best was her "special delivery" brown poodle. It came from somewhere but nobody really could say where. My mother went gaga over Princess Bonnie which is what she named her. I was not too keen on the dog. It seemed to have a very hyper personality so I never took it for a walk. I never did anything with Bonnie.

One afternoon I walked over to my grandmother's back porch. She had sheets hanging on the clothesline.

I felt something behind me. It was Bonnie. The sheets blew in the wind and Bonnie freaked and as I turned around she jumped up on me and bit my left wrist. I screamed. My grandmother ran outside. My father came from the ranch house and lifted me in his arms and took me home. I woke up in my parents' bed. I had fainted when Bonnie bit me. I recovered, but Bonnie was sent away immediately. My mother held it against me for years. I stared at my seven-year-old scar on my left wrist and never forgot the pain of being bitten.

# SALAMANDER

ONE MORNING MY mother looked out the picture window and saw elephants lumbering down Congress Street tail to tail. Every few minutes they would let out their happy trumpeting. It was the circus coming to town.

I was dropped off at the Bolivar field. I am not sure who was with me, if anyone. I walked excitedly under the big tents and saw all the clowns with their big red mouths and stringy hair and red noses.

The sawdust was soft under my feet. But it made me sneeze. Just before it was time to leave I stopped at a booth selling salamanders. I picked out a little white box and brought it home. Once home I took the white box to the vortex. There I opened the little box and there inside was something alive. Its small eyes looked right at me. I lifted it out and held its cool skin in my hand. The little green salamander fascinated me for days. When it was time to go inside for the night I placed the little box between a crack in the stone wall along the vortex.

One day the little salamander turned brown. I wasn't sure what it meant. I didn't ask anyone. I knew leaves turned colors like orange and yellow and red and then they became dull and brown.

A few more weeks went by and I visited my salamander in the first snow. There inside the little box was a black and stiff salamander. I gasped and felt sick. The food that came with the box was gone. I didn't know how to get more. Winter came with a vengeance. I didn't know what to do with my dead salamander. I would get in trouble if I took him inside.

I had messed up. This sweet green salamander with eyes that looked right at me was now frozen and gone. At my young age I had no one to tell me about the cycle of life and death. I had to learn all alone. I never bought another salamander from the circus.

# THE BIRDS AND
# THE BEES

MY MOTHER BROUGHT a small library booklet on *the birds and the bees* into my sister's large bedroom and asked me to join her. Apparently, she felt coming into my small room was too crowded for her. She lay on my sister's full-size mattress stretched out on her right side holding this little booklet.

I looked from my standing position and thought I saw flowers in greens and yellows. I had no desire to sit on my sister's bed so I kept standing and my mother did not invite me to join her.

My mother's doe-like brown eyes seemed to contemplate other worlds at times which I could never understand. She kept the booklet close to her with her strong hands.

"This talks about birds and flowers and bees. Do you know about that?"

Did I know about what? I wondered.

There was a long silence.

"Well, you can read this now when you want to."

She did not extend it to me. She kept holding it to her own body.

"I'll leave it here and you can take it into your room. There are pictures of pretty flowers."

She put the booklet down and got up.

She passed by me but did not touch me.

She left the room.

I leaned gingerly toward the booklet. I wanted to tell my mother about the robin's nest I saw on the third-floor window ledge of my grandmother's house. The nest was magical...to look and see three small, round, blue eggs protected by the mother robin. She was busy flying back and forth around the birch tree gathering food for her babies. They would soon hatch.

Now I had this booklet to read. I picked it up and got out of my little sister's room fast. I slid open the gray plastic door then shut it quickly behind me. I felt safe inside my small bedroom.

I sat on my little twin bed and opened the booklet.

Yes, there were pictures of birds and flowers and some word I did not know "stamen."

*What does that mean?* I wondered. I closed the booklet and never asked a single question of my mother.

I went over to my desk and began to trace pictures of Eeyore!

# DANCE

BALLET AND TAP dancing were taught to little girls at the Graham studio on Congress Street. It was three houses up the street from my family's ranch. The two men who ran the studio, Roger and Terry, were known to be homosexuals; the only ones in town in the fifties. No one called them 'gay' since that word had not grown into its new entomology. My grandmother always used the word 'gay' to mean fun or amusing.

Roger taught the dance classes and Terry had a millinery room full of hats he designed and sewed. My grandmother often looked at his fine creations when she needed a new hat.

I was never sent up the street for dance lessons. I never crammed my feet into pink ballet slippers or black toe shoes tapping away or stretching into a Plie.

What I began to realize as a little girl was my father did not want me near two men who lived together. Years later, what struck me as wondrous strange was the fact that the night my grandmother died, at age 93, was spent with Roger and Terry. They enjoyed a fun night drinking and socializing with Martinis until my grandmother collapsed at their home. The ambulance came and took her to the hospital. My beloved grandmother died that very night in the hospital. The men left town soon after and were never heard from again.

# EVANS ROLLER RINK

A COUPLE OWNED the roller-skating rink on the other side of town. It was the Saturday afternoon hang out for many, many girls. Getting your scruffy torn worn rented roller skates on your feet meant hilarious fun in the moody dark rink. Colored lights hung all around and from the ceiling a round ball was blinking on and off in a very psychedelic way.

Girls and more girls circled the rink joining hands and arms together. Round and round and round to the '50s music. When the circling got repetitive to great songs like "There Goes My Baby," Mack the Knife," "Volare", "Great Balls of Fire," Splish Splash," "Venus," and "Smoke Gets In Your Eyes', the music changed to the "Hokey Pokey."

"Put your right hand in; put your right hand out .........You do the Hokey Pokey and you turn yourself about"!!! The place was laughter, skinned knees, and worn-out skates. What couldn't be seen was the dream of every young girl to own her own pair of new white roller skates with blue pompoms.

# FOOD

ONE RULE INSIDE the house was we were not allowed to leave the table until we finished everything on our plate. I couldn't stomach many of the vegetables that were cooked from a can: peas, corn, beets, carrots. I often sat through dinner eating in silence until it was time to excuse myself and go do the dishes.

Whenever it became obvious I was not going to eat my vegetables I was sent to the kitchen to eat soggy white bread and milk.

Food was not something that brought joy to my taste buds. I remember every sugary cereal on the market and our table; Sugar Corn Pops, which I eventually fed the white ducks and Tony the Tiger, Frosted Flakes. White Wonder Bread with peanut butter and jelly was a staple along with Campbell's tomato soup and Kraft grilled cheese sandwiches.

At night there were TV dinners, hamburgers, and meatloaf with a piece of hearts of lettuce topped with a mayo and ketchup dressing. Never fresh salads. No big steaks or roasts ever came out of the oven. We did get a turkey at Christmas and Thanksgiving.

My grandmother would bring over a Waldorf salad many nights. My mother loved to make Jello with bananas just like so many other housewives did in the 1950s.

The only fun night was Friday when we ate fried fish, French fries, and coleslaw served at every restaurant in town. My father would bring the order home and we would breathe a sigh of relief at the greasy meal. It was the one moment being Catholic had its advantages since fish was required on Fridays. Desserts were ice cream, sherbet, Drumsticks, or packaged Archway cookies.

# QUIET

THERE WERE QUIET hours in the ranch house that I often did not understand. I often found myself alone in the house without a clue about where my three brothers and little sister had gone. When I was around seven or eight my mother would pester me about everything whenever she saw me. She would ask me questions I could not answer. She would sound sarcastic and it frightened me. When she raised her voice I would sometimes yell right back at her and then she would come at me with the dreaded soap. Soap in my mouth and then she told me to sit in the closet in the boys' room on the first floor with the chair facing toward the blank white wall. I sat there looking at the white walls trying to figure out what question I had failed to answer. I knew

I could swear right back at her but that was only because she had agitated me to respond and stand up for my rights against her cruelty. Her questions were often phrased with a *What do you know about*? It seemed to be some gossip or fact she wanted me to verify for her so she didn't feel left in the dark. My answer was always, *I don't know anything.*

When my father got home on one of those days and he asked if my mother had a good day she would answer, 'Mary was naughty.'

I was taken upstairs to my parents' bedroom. My father closed the door. He bent me over his lap and took the nearby hairbrush and spanked me with it.

I never heard that my brothers were punished like this. I never witnessed my father spanking my little sister in all those years. I never said a word to my siblings. I still cannot remember how many times I was sent to my parents' bedroom. It did eventually end, but the internal scars were kept as wounds forever.

I began to develop the habit of running away from the house to the 'bumpy tracks' (my name for the flagstones running down the length of my grandmother's house on the Dorn side of her home). I found my favorite pine tree and laid down with my flashlight.

Whenever I was outside a fearful hush spread over my little patch of earth around my parents' home. Would my parents settle down from their meanness and fighting? Would my own fear subside enough that I could go back inside and go to my bed?

I felt calm near my grandmother's home but I did not go running inside crying to her. I didn't want to bother her and it was all too shameful to reveal. Besides, I knew my grandmother stayed out of my parents' upbringing of their children. Her home remained a haven of love and beauty all those years I was hiding under the pine tree.

# INDIAN BURIAL

MY FATHER TOOK us on Sunday afternoon rides quite often. And just as often car sickness set in and remarks about wanting to stay home. But this particular afternoon intrigued me. We lived 10 miles from Salamanca, New York which was owned by Seneca Indians. My father drove. I sat in the back seat behind him and looked at his brown hair. He drove to the area where Chief Cornplanter, of the Seneca tribe, was buried. The Senecas had made many treaties with the white man that the white man broke.

We drove somewhere down some road with nothing all around. No signs or stores or villages. It was empty land.

My father stopped the car and told us to look across the road. There were large black tarps hung up with poles.

"What's that for?" my mother asked.

"They're digging up Indians from their sacred burial grounds."

"Why?"

"Because they feel like it. They're building a dam and reservoir here for power all the way to Pittsburgh. And they don't give a damn."

My stomach got very upset. I thought I might throw up. I got out of the car and took a deep breath of the painterly blue sky.

My father stood by me.

"I just thought you should see this."

I looked out again at the black tarps. I was angry at this injustice to the Seneca Indians and I was only nine or ten.

We drove away in silence. Ordinarily on

Sundays we ended up at Neilly's for home-made ice cream. You could see the cows near the barn. My father took me in one afternoon and I had the chance to milk a cow. It was thrilling!

There was no ice cream cone that Sunday afternoon. I wanted to go home and be safe from government diggers and this huge betrayal of the Seneca Indians.

# TUBBERS

TUBBERS WERE A Bradford invention. A man named Ray "Tubber" Sheehan invented them in 1917. A "Tubber" consisted of vanilla ice cream, marshmallow fluff, chocolate syrup, and salty Mexican peanuts.

They were still around when I was a child in the 1950s. On Saturday afternoons following a matinee at the Dipson theatre I walked next door to Galinis' diner and ate a Tubber. There were cream-colored mushy-soft booths and a counter with stools inside the diner. My mother loved Tubbers and sometimes she would join my little sister and me at Galinis.

Just about the moment when I thought this was the greatest way to spend a Saturday afternoon, watching a Disney movie and eating a Tubber, my mother changed the rules.

Now I was being forced to go out with a girl I did not know to Galinis to eat a Tubber. My mother chose the young, pretty, (according to my mother) rich girl. She was the daughter of a woman my mother knew from her bridge club. She telephoned Mrs. Mackey to arrange for Patricia to meet me at Galinis. My little sister was out of the picture.

I was embarrassed down to my feet. I did not know the girl and she was older. Patricia was fourteen or fifteen, from a rich doctor's family who lived across town in the Interstate Parkway area near the hospital.

I was dropped off at Galanis.

"I'll pick you up at five," my mother told me with a strong hand on my back as she gave me a push.

Horrified! Mortified! Crucified!. I was not even twelve yet.

I walked in slowly. There was Patricia, all dressed up in a dress and flats and sweater for Saturday Tubber time. She wore a gold circle pin. I wore my favorite Indian jacket, pants, a sweater and my Buster Brown shoes.

I believe Patricia did all the talking. I don't remember speaking a word. I ate. Slurping all the gooey sugar up into my mouth to please my mother.

I'm not sure Patricia even ordered a Tubber. She might have had a piece of pie or a scoop of ice cream in a dish. And a Coke. Two water glasses sat on the table. And who paid for this embarrassing social time?

When I saw Patricia take her last sip of Coke I blurted out:

"What time is it?"

"Five minutes to five. Are you getting a ride home?"

She was kind.

"Yes, my mother is coming."

And that was the end of Patricia in my life.

A few weeks later it turned more mortifying. My mother got the bright idea she would call her childhood friend Julie, who was married to David Dorn, and ask her to bring Brooks to our house. Brooks? Her daughter? Brooks was a Dorn! Drop-dead gorgeous and extraordinary! But all of them were like that. They were the daughters of people who were beautiful, powerful, rich and adventurous. They left their small frog pond and took their lives to the biggest state in the country, Texas. They must have gotten some message that their beauty and looks gave them power not to mention their oil heritage.

When Brooks turned fifteen she came into her inheritance of looks and power. She had long eyelashes that were blond and long blond hair she wore in braids. She smelled good. She had a perfect body and she was good at horseback riding. She had won ribbons at the Valley Hunt Club whenever she entered the horse shows.

I had learned all through childhood that oil was power and rich was the layer of living that I would not enter. But it was always fun to watch their power and beauty arrive each summer in Dorn's driveway.

Julie accepted my mother's invitation for Brooks. The next thing I knew I was going to entertain this beauty.

"The house will be better," my mother said, "more friendly."

I looked at my mother like she had lost her mind.

This ranch? She lives in a mansion in Texas and an estate at Glendorn and next door is her grandmother's fine opulent home, I thought to myself.

We are in a ranch. The cheap French doors look out at her grandmother's home across our back yard. I guess that fact was what my mother was hoping would keep Brooks here more than five minutes.

She arrived in a pretty, fashionable dress.

My mother had all the fixings for the Tubber in the kitchen where we were supposed to get in line and help ourselves. Brooks very graciously got her Tubber but she asked if she could skip the Mexican peanuts, they didn't agree with her.

"Of course," my mother said.

If I had told my mother I did not want the Mexican peanuts she would have force-fed them down my throat.

The whole devious plan to force me to entertain a DORN was going well. My mother sent me a sinister smile inferring 'I told you so.'

We walked into the dining room where a card table stood in the corner. My mother had placed a pretty tablecloth over the table.

Brooks sat down with her Tubber.

"Oh, I see my grandmother's home over there."

My mother picked up on the conversation and informed Brooks that she and her mother Julie were childhood friends.

Brooks was lovely. Brooks was gracious. Brooks showed perfect manners. Brooks made conversation with my mother who never left the room. I was partially glad she didn't and partially wished she would vanish just to test my own conversation acumen at eleven with this magnificent creature.

I never saw Brooks again. With her inheritance of oil and beauty she began to come less frequently to the Bradford Glendorn estate. It was time for her to find boys to love.

Besides, the rules dictated that a Dorn grandchild was never going to be friends with a Bradford child, ever. They stayed among themselves and had plenty of cousins with names like Clayton, Tucker, Leslie, Daly, Forest and Brooks.

# DENNY

I WAS ELEVEN when I experienced my first rejection by a boy. It was the year I endured a teacher named Miss Napolitan in the split classroom (fifth and sixth graders together). Long red nails, red lipstick, brown mousy hair down to her shoulders, long straight skirts with a tight sweater and a scarf tied at her neck. And high heels. She wore thick glasses that did not flatter her face. Her glamour effect was lost by the glasses. She arrived in town one year and left the next. It seemed many young teachers did that while I was growing up.

Miss Napolitan was in charge of both the fifth and sixth graders in one room. The fifth graders' desks all faced the blackboard on one side and the sixth graders all circled around Miss Napolitan in chairs.

I never met Denny formally but I saw him everyday sitting next to Miss Napolitan as the teacher's pet. All the sixth-grade girls had a crush on him. I wanted to be part of that circle of girls that included Molly. I slipped a note to Molly and asked her to slip it to Denny.

Want to meet me at Elm and Congress today after school?

He told Molly to tell me "Sure."

I was so excited. My hand was cramped from writing spelling words 100 times for Miss Napolitan; this is how she disciplined her fifth graders for a whole year. But a cramped hand could not keep me from the excitement I felt about a date with Denny.

I waited at the corner. He approached. His hair was all slicked back like Elvis Presley. He had a square face and dishwater blond hair. His eyes were piercing blue. He seemed to have muscles where the other boys didn't. He seemed to scorch the sidewalk with his cool walk and look.

He seemed to know girls thought he was good-looking. I wasn't sure but I guess he smoked. And when he had gathered with some of his hunky friends at Smith's Market I had noticed the girls giggling when the boys made a dirty sign with their middle finger.

The sixth-grade girls were walking slowly past the corner and across the street to go to the market for pop. Everyone knew about this meeting between Denny and me.

I felt like I was going to faint. I'm not sure what I could have said, being shy about this whole thing now that it was happening.

What did we say?

"Hey."

"Hey."

"Want to walk me home?"

"Yeah."

He walked me up the street to 126 Congress Street and by that time we were going to go on a date to the movies on Friday.

I walked up the driveway.

"See ya," he said.

He walked on. I stopped and hid behind the stone wall to see if he doubled back to the market where his friends were hanging out.

He didn't.

I had Friday to look forward to. My mother had okayed this date which was very uncharacteristic of her. She didn't put me through the third degree but just asked for his name and how I knew him.

My older brother waited with me in my sister's bedroom. It had the best hidden view. We both looked down the curvy driveway. Denny was coming at 6:30 p.m. for the 7 o'clock movie.

I wore something pretty. I was so proud I had a date with Denny. Me. A fifth grader going out with the teacher's pet. I thought for sure God was with me in this moment.

Twilight began to drop behind the hills. My parents seemed oblivious watching TV downstairs. My brother stood quietly by the window.

It was 6:45 p.m. and no young man was walking up the driveway in the blue hour. My sweater began to feel tight around my waist.

I looked at my brother. He kept watching.

The clock read 7 p.m. in the hallway.

Where is he?

My brother's face let me know that this can happen with boys.

By 7:15 p.m. I had to accept the truth. He was not coming. I never got a phone call from Denny and his mother never called my mother.

I had no reason to go on. I had been diminished to nothingness at age eleven. There would be no sweet dark in the theater; no Denny putting his arm around my shoulder; no sharing of popcorn. The experience left me with disturbing thoughts the rest of my fifth-grade year.

When I saw Denny in class the next week I avoided looking at him which was easy to do since our desks were still facing away from the sixth graders toward the wall.

When I finally sneaked a look at him I suddenly saw him as a greasy Elvis Presley and I liked Pat Boone with his white bucks. In fact, I had a picture on my bedroom wall of Pat Boone to look at that evening.

Denny was a loser from that day forward though he had set off a bomb of desire in my heart. It was over. I gave him up as fast as lightning.

I kept my back to his world and kept writing my spelling words 100 times with the rest of my fifth-grade classmates.

I always felt embarrassed by the whole incident around my mother. I had begged her to let me go on a date with this boy. Yet I could not step out into the big world of boys without this rejection. My mother never spoke a word about it to me.

Still, I knew it was important, one of those big moments that seeps down inside you and never leaves. I was years away from sex or getting drunk or going off to college but it was still a big deal for a young innocent eleven year old. He was the first boy since Rexy Rogers and he rejected me.

The following weeks I thought he looked like a baby sitting next to Miss Napolitan, as she let him play teacher's pet.

# SUMMER

SUMMER MEANT THE Valley Hunt Club for most of my childhood. It started with the Memorial Day Parade. My father left early to find a parking space for the car. He stopped off at Johnson's for breakfast. The owners were Greek but they had changed their names to fit in with what America expected in a name.

My father found the closest parking meter near the corner of Congress and Main. He was very familiar with this Memorial Day Parade. He had led the Navy Veterans down Main in his white uniform in '46, '47 and '48, after World War II.

When he walked in the front door we were all ready with our swimsuits and towels all packed in bags. My mother and siblings walked down Congress Street to the car where we sat on the hood. The parade began at 10. It started off with the Veterans of Foreign Wars, then the firetrucks, then floats and bands playing patriotic songs. We waved and clapped for everyone.

The moment it ended my father turned on the ignition and off we went down Congress Street to Lewis Run, and then a right to the Valley Hunt Club. One had to join the club and become a member in order to swim and ride horses and play tennis. My parents had joined when they were first married.

It was heaven to run from the car into the girls' dressing room, throw on my swimsuit then run outside to the pool and jump in. I spent the rest of Memorial Day in the water except for lunch at the snack bar where I ate my usual cheeseburger, potato chips and Orange Crush. Nothing was on my mind but the air in the hills and the wide blue pool where my body splashed and swam and dove off the diving board until my muscles had to rest. Swim and rest and eat and swim and rest and eat. Nothing interfered with this pattern of summer at the Valley Hunt Club for many years.

# PART II

# THE BACKSTROKE

WHAT THE DORNS had besides a magnificent full-size pool was an Olympic diving instructor who was in charge of all the grandchildren learning to swim and dive.

My swimming lesson came from my father. I remember being held for a few minutes in the shallow end of the Valley Hunt Club pool and let go very soon after. I took to the water like a fish. I taught myself to do the free-style and backstroke.

One summer the Valley Hunt Club decided to have a swim meet. I was probably eleven. The Dorns were going to compete in it. They were going to leave Glendorn for the day and come to the Club. Their instructor would accompany them. All the kids who swam every day at the Club were totally excited.

I had picked the backstroke as my favorite stroke. But even though there was a lifeguard he never taught me to do the somersault turn at the wall. I just touched and turned topside. I entered my name for backstroke competition. Several Dorn girls entered the same race.

The meet ran all day. The Dorns did very well in the diving competition and their instructor was pleased.

The backstroke race was next. I was in the water at the shallow end with my back to the deep end. There was a Dorn to my left and right and further right. Three Dorns and me. The race was down to the deep end turn and back to the shallow end (50 yards).

My little sister was my biggest fan. She stood near the edge of the pool ready to cheer for me.

"On your mark, get set, GO!"

I pushed off into my own lane and swam my favorite stroke down to the deep end stroking with my arms and legs…turned at the end and pushed off to the shallow. Kicking! Kicking! Pulling… pulling…breathing hard to the wall where my hand touched first.

The whistle blew. I was the winner! Beating all three Dorns trained by an instructor!

The lifeguard presented me with a small medal with Valley Hunt Club on it. Or maybe not. I cannot remember the medal. My sister clapped and clapped and jumped up and down. I could hardly believe my body had done such a wonderful thing in the water. I had beat the Dorns with my own backstroke.

# FATHER'S CHRISTMAS PRESENT

WHEN I WAS eleven or twelve I got the idea I'd give my father something special for Christmas. I guess I had some money from babysitting two little boys that were the sons of an insurance agent my father knew. My grandmother had helped me open a Christmas savings account which made me very happy. The gift for my father would take all of my money so my grandmother was going to help me buy smaller gifts for the rest of the family.

I walked into Leshner's Mens Store under the Emery Hotel at the foot of Main Street on a beautiful snowy evening in December. It was dark but I was allowed to walk alone down Congress to Main because Bradford was safe in the 1950s. Main Street twinkled with Christmas lights and wreaths hung on every pole. Music filled the air and snow falling from the sky touched my tongue when I opened my mouth. All the windows were decorated with magical old-fashioned Christmas toys and Christmas scenes.

I opened the door to Leshners. A bell jingled. A salesman came over to me. He looked surprised at my young age. I walked quietly around the store fingering the fine wools and cotton shirts with holes for cufflinks. Then I saw them. Smoking jackets. Beautiful deep blue velvet smoking jackets with satin lapels.

I gasped because I knew I had found the perfect gift. I reached up on my toes.

"Is this what you want?"

"Yes, please."

The salesman helped me bring down the hanger and jacket.

I felt the material. So elegant.

"Do you think my Dad will like this? He doesn't smoke."

"Oh, he doesn't have to smoke. What's your Dad's name?"

"Mr. Keating."

"Why I know him well. No need to be a smoker. He can wear it just to be comfortable in the evening. "

I'd never seen my father in anything but his work clothes and sweaters. This jacket was so beyond anything I could have ever dreamed up. It spoke to me.

"I'll take it."

"I think he might be a large. And this is his size."

"I measured his jackets at home so I'd know." I handed him the numbers on a small slip of paper.

"Very good young lady."

The salesman smiled. We walked to the counter. He wrapped the jacket in tissue paper and then he placed it in the black and gold box with Leshner's logo on it.

I handed him my money. He wished me a Merry Christmas.

When I walked up the driveway to the house I entered the back cellar stairs that led to my small bedroom. I hid the beautiful box under my twin bed.

When Christmas morning came my gift was the last one opened by anyone. The room was hushed.

My father removed the tissue paper. He found the indigo blue smoking jacket inside. His eyes glistened. He didn't speak but he tried it on. It fit perfectly. He turned around for my mother to see all sides of him.

He kept it on all Christmas evening.

I dreamt happily that Christmas night of all the lovely presents given and received but most of all of the memory of my father in his new smoking jacket. When he quietly tiptoed into my bedroom I was barely awake but I remember his kiss on my cheek.

Years later when my father died he was buried in his indigo velvet smoking jacket which still fit him after 40 years! He never missed wearing it Christmas day and night all those many years.

# BLEEDING AT BONNYBROOK

"MOM I'M BLEEDING," I announced one morning as she was walking down the hallway to the bathroom. I stood in the doorway of my sister's room.

"I told you about that."

Did she? I didn't remember much about the conversation.

"Yeah, but I can't go to E's birthday party now. I can't."

"Of course you can. You're going!"

It was August and E's twelfth birthday party

at Bonnybrook. Bonnybrook was her family's summer place a few miles past the Pennhills Club outside Bradford. Deep within the pine trees a 1930s large cottage painted in pale green, their summer retreat, occupied the moist dense land. They had a swimming pool in the front. E lived in this wealthy world because E's father was an oil producer.

I loved to swim but I couldn't swim in a Kotex. I had it stuffed in me under my blue gym shorts which I despised.

When I arrived around dusk, the guests were all standing around a big family table eating junk food. Jeanette, E's housekeeper, was bringing in fresh drinks and the tray with the cake and ice cream on it.

I walked to the table, shamed and self-conscious of my bulging body dressed in the god-awful gym shorts. I ate junk food and then I went outside to the pool.

I am sure it was fun singing "Happy Birthday" to E and eating cake and ice cream but I only remember two things from the night.

I stood by the pool while all the girls jumped in the water and splashed around and played games and laughed and had a fun time. There I stood cemented to the patio never budging toward the water in the pool. I wanted that water in the pool, yet I couldn't go in. The screams of delight only heightened my suffering from the blood now running down through the insides of me out to the big bloody Kotex.

Swimming at night in a pool was magical and I was missing the whole moment.

Later when it was time for bed E asked me to join her in her own bedroom. There were two twin beds end to end in the wood-paneled room. E was in one and I was in the other. Our feet were facing each other, nearly touching. I now felt a little more comfortable in my pajamas over my underwear and Kotex.

I settled down against the pillow and was about to fall into a deep sleep. But then I heard E telling me about babies.

She was explaining where they came from.

She knew I had my first period.

"Look they come from in here."

With a quick flick of her nightgown she lifted it above her knees and spread her young legs and pointed with her index finger.

"In here!"

I was stunned. It was so bold of E to show me physically and it was so compassionate to teach me what my mother had not.

"Oh," I muttered. "I gotta sleep."

I sank into the pillow. I wanted to fall into a deep deep sleep that would erase the last few minutes, maybe the last few days since my period started. I wanted to feel my bloodless body swimming in that deliciously cool water with the magic of the lights reflecting the night above. I wanted to be part of the party and play and splash with the other twelve-year-old girls at Bonnybrook!

# SHOPPING – FIRST BRA

ONCE IT BECAME obvious to my mother (not me) that I needed to tuck my new breasts into a bra I was sent off to Main Street. I loved Main Street stores that could answer any dream you desired. I loved Barnsdall's store where fancy pens in a glass case drew me toward them in a swoon of desire.

But I was not on my way to buy a pen. I was on my way to Johnston's which was the ladies store on Main. It was so fancy they had pneumatic tubes that whisked your bill upstairs to accounting and then flew it back in the tube to the friendly saleswoman. I went in and someone who smelled nice and wore pretty clothes and earrings and lipstick came over to me. I touched the nightgowns and slips and saw many undies spread over the sturdy wooden cabinets. The ceiling was tin and from the second-floor windows the sun sprinkled the merchandise with particles of light.

She selected a few white bras and showed me into a dressing room. I think I was a 32 B then. Hardly recognizing what was happening to me with the mysterious hormones that had arrived, I put my growing breasts into the cups. This was not a mother/daughter moment.

At that moment, hidden behind the curtain, I wished for my cousin V-Anne who was one of four red-haired Irish sisters. She would be able to help me. We were the same age and cousins by great grandmothers through marriage. The word 'cousin' was fun for me to say since both my parents were only children. I never had aunts or uncles or first cousins.

But distant cousins did not turn out well for my older brother who dated V-Anne's sister. He was handsome and she was gorgeous with that Irish red hair and anyone could see they were intensely in love. They both played the clarinet in the high school band and they used to meet at the drugstore in town and drink cherry cokes after school. But someone told me that because they were distant cousins by marriage they could not marry. It nearly broke my brother's heart when he was forced to listen to gossip and meddlers in town. They were not blood relations at all but fifth cousins. No marriage between my older brother and V-Anne's sister was very sad.

All these thoughts went through my mind when I looked at the two white cups on me. The saleswoman called in "Everything fit?"

"Yes."

I took 'it' out to her and she put it in a pretty bag with tissue paper. I handed her the cash. Then I stood mesmerized again by the pneumatic tube whisking the bill and money away.

I walked out of Johnston's wishing I had the money for a good Sheaffer pen at Barnsdall's Office Supply Store.

# BIG BEDROOM DOWNSTAIRS

WHEN I WAS thirteen I moved out of my little room to the downstairs room my brothers had used. They moved upstairs to the re-modeled attic room that held all three twin beds and a large desk for homework.

With old brown linoleum floors, white walls and four closets staring at her, my mother became a home decorator. She hired the best designers in the area: Wellman Brothers of Jamestown, NY and began to turn her ideas into a reality.

What I remember about the downstairs room where my brothers slept was my toy rock-ing horse I named Trigger. I rode him when

I was five. I rocked and rocked so much that my older brother stood amazed by my energy: my mother joined him and stared at her bundle of little girl that wanted nothing but to ride Trigger.

The linoleum floor disappeared. A wall-to-wall blue carpet replaced it. The men went in and wallpapered with big, bold, blue flowers with matching drapes. A chaise lounge with the curtain fabric sat in the corner. Bookcases that my father painted in a soft aquamarine to match the fabric appeared. A full-size bed with a custom-made bedspread finished the pulled together "house and garden" look.

I moved into the room and never looked back. There was a small bathroom next to my room that I shared with my youngest brother now that my older brothers had left for college.

I was no longer cramped in my 7 x 9 foot room with the ugly partition and the path that sent me through my sister's room just to go to the bathroom. I did not have to tiptoe anymore. I was free and I loved it. I no longer looked out at the curvy driveway to the street. Now my window looked right out at the pretty flowered back yard and my grandmother's house.

What I do regret are the treasures from my small bedroom that seemed to disappear in the move. I did not have Bozo, the clown, or Zippy, the chimpanzee, or Lassie, or my painted bird models in the new bedroom. My father threw everything away he considered junk. All my play things fell into that junk category.

He dismantled his Lionel Train set. It was his pride and joy. He set up the incredible large track on a huge piece of plywood in the attic. The train circled the entire room with that magical sound of the whistle. There were cows and dairy stops and a conductor and trees and bridges and snow. Magical. It was so wonderful to see my father move the lever and watch the train go 'round and 'round. But he never played with his sons and they never once played with the train. It was rather sad. He dismantled it one day and that was the end of the whistle and the priceless Lionel train set.

I rescued the book *Winnie the Pooh* and my record player from the garbage. Now I was in my menstruation bedroom. My mother was elated at the results of her decorating. I had not chosen anything for the new bedroom I was to occupy for six years.

# SCHOOL STREET / SENIOR HIGH

THE GIRLS IN school wore gold circle pins and loafers, pleated Pendleton skirts, Peter Pan blouses and sweaters. They sometimes smelled like Shalimar. I remember wearing a poodle skirt for a few days. But I mostly wore blouses with mohair sweaters over them. And some kind of straight skirt. I loved wearing loafers. I even wanted cleats on mine like the shop boys wore while hanging out smoking cigarettes. But I got a big 'no' from my mother!

I liked going to school. I liked the bells ringing for change of classes; the rush of all the great kids hurrying down the hallways; the buzz of conversation. I don't remember much in the way of learning. I seemed to breeze through most of my classes. Though geometry in seventh grade did set me back. But my mother had studied it at Shipley and she helped me draw the shapes and do the math every night. It was one of the few times I understood my mother. She was a very good teacher of geometry and she had retained all of it from boarding school twenty-five years earlier.

We often went on field trips right in town since Bradford had Zippo, Dresser, and Kendall Oil in the fifties.

The guidance counselors divided us up into groups with names we never forgot: General, Vocational, Business, and College Prep. I was in College Prep with no idea where I wanted to go or why. For five years I wandered the halls of School Street taking all of my classes. Since there were so many kids in my senior class they decided to renovate the old senior high school. It was totally shut down for two years. Our classes were split between morning and afternoon shifts for two years at the old junior high school. It changed the tone and structure of our lives. What do we do with half a day off we never expected? One was free of structure but we were robbed of two years with our classmates in the halls of senior high.

Many of the guys hung out smoking and doing nothing. Some of the girls got part-time jobs at the telephone company. I got a job as a secretary with my father in the insurance firm where he was an agent. Since I was not in the Business Group I had no typing or business math or bookkeeping skills, all subjects that would have been helpful.

Somehow we all got through the two years of chaos to become the first graduating class from the newly renovated senior high school. We had a spanking new cafeteria and a brand new theater that seated a thousand. The desks and chairs were all new. The PA system was new. The shop and vocational areas were all new. The library was new. We graduated 412 seniors in 1966. Because we were the first to graduate from the new senior high school we were the proudest senior class ever to walk the halls of Bradford High!

# GONE WITH THE WIND

*GONE WITH THE Wind* came to town at the Dipson theatre when I was 12. I went to see it with Molly. Molly lived on Clarence Street and she was in the fifth and sixth split grade with Miss Napolitan. She was a sixth grader. We met walking up Congress Street and knew each other from our class together. Clarence Street was a long walk as a child but we never seemed to mind. We passed 126 Congress to Kane Street and Pike and Sherman where we turned right, then left to 117 Clarence. Molly invited me into her home. I was excited to be going to the movie with my own little friend. This was not a set-up arranged by my mother. I had found Molly all by myself and that made me feel less crazy in her company. Molly and I had fun all the time. We never fought or felt we had done something to hurt each other. There were no misunderstandings.

Molly's bedroom was on the second floor. It was comfortable without an ornateness about it. I think I may have secretly wanted to sleep there for the night after seeing the movie.

It seemed that I had heard of *Gone With The Wind* for months from my mother who saw it when she was nineteen in the year it was released, 1939. It was twenty years later.

She told me over and over how all the women movie stars auditioned for the part of Scarlett O'Hara and how they found Vivien Leigh the night they were burning the sets for the Atlanta fire. I had a program from my mother's 1939 keepsakes. I loved looking at the pictures of the stars like Clark Gable and Olivia de Havilland. I had not read the book yet, but my mother had several times.

When Molly and I sat on the right side of the theatre in seats near the front I had no idea what I was in for. Once the music started with

Tara's theme I felt something inside me move and never go back.

Then I saw Scarlett O'Hara! And Tara!

When Scarlett's mother died and Scarlett let out her scream I got off my seat and crouched down on the floor. I stayed there until Scarlett pulled the carrots up from the red earth of Tara and stood up with her famous speech: "As God as my witness, I'll never go hungry again!" By this time Molly was concerned but didn't drag me up. She didn't make me feel odd about being on the floor. I got up on my own when I could.

The thought of my mother dying at any time in the universal cosmos of time was unacceptable to me. I kept that scream, the same as Scarlett's, inside me for the rest of my life. On the day my own mother died, in my arms, I released it.

After getting back home I had to go to bed. Later my older brother ordered a beautiful hardbound copy of *Gone With The Wind* that came to the front door in a "special delivery."

A few days later another "special delivery" package came for me and it was from my other older brother. He sent me the original soundtrack to *Gone With The Wind*.

Later in the year Molly and I would hide out in places in her house or back yard or my house and back yard and we would read all the romantic and sad passages between Ashley and Scarlett and Scarlett and Rhett.

Thus began my whole new interest in the Civil War. I bought books on all the famous battles and Sherman's "March to the Sea." It kept me away from the whole family for a whole year while I read and read and read. I had biographies of Clark Gable and Vivien Leigh that piqued my twelve-year-old heart.

What I did notice was my father never said one word to me about my new passion.

He never said a thing about the Irish father in the movie. He never said a thing about the Irish plantation called Tara.

I knew that my father was Irish but because

he never uttered a syllable about his Irishness I said nothing either. I knew that my paternal grandfather was Irish and had come from Ireland but since he disappeared from my life and our family over some cruel situation my father never forgave I had no Irish to see or hear or feel. I never heard *Danny Boy* or *When Irish Eyes Are Smiling*. I never heard a story about Ireland.

I remember the Irish 'Pa' in *Gone With The Wind* took Scarlett to the mound of Tara and looked out at the land:

*"Land is the only thing in the world that amounts to anything," he shouted, his thick short arms making wide gestures of indignation, "for tis the only thing in this world that lasts, and don't you be forgetting it! Tis the only thing worth working for, worth fighting for -- worth dying for."*

And then: *"And don't be forgetting that you are half Irish, Miss! And to anyone with a drop of Irish blood in them the land they live on is like their mother."*

I ached and longed for my father to give me some of that Irish heritage pulsing in my blood.

After the movie red earth was what I wanted. I had no idea where Ireland really was in the geography of the world. I wanted red earth though. I wanted to grow into loving the land. When I looked around me with my young eyes I did not see anything that resembled red earth. Not one blade of grass, or flower or birch tree resembled what my twelve-year-old eyes saw in the Irish Tara in *Gone With The Wind*. And my father hid his Irishness from me rather than be proud like Gerald O'Hara.

# GYM CLASS

THE MORTIFYING, HATED blue gym shorts and blousy top was too much to endure but there it was. Dressing next to girls in front of lockers was a blank to me. I cannot remember who dressed or undressed next to me. I don't even remember dragging myself into the shower stalls. What does remain is the memory of the gym teacher.

Her name was Mrs. Hoffman. I never saw her husband. She came from one of those small Pennsylvania colleges. She had a Buster Brown hair cut for her dark black, salt and pepper hair. She had a strong square chin that jutted out, thin lips, wide smile and blue eyes. Her laugh was a full throaty sound that reverberated down the hallways of Junior High on School Street.

In gym class we did the required leaps over the horse and parallel bars and played basketball. Basketball was my favorite, but it soon drizzled away as none of the other girls were very good at it. I had breathed basketball in my own home court for years on Congress Street.

Meeting up again with Molly in Junior High School rekindled our friendship. Molly and I began to take a huge school-girl interest in Mrs. Hoffman's favorite student, Judy. It occupied our minds during class breaks and lunches in the cafeteria.

Judy was not overweight and she probably would head for Radcliffe or somewhere in Boston when she graduated. She had a really wide mouth with big teeth and short dishwater blond hair. She wore loafers and skirts and Peter Pan blouses with sweaters all week. She was two years ahead of me and one year ahead of Molly which put her in the 9th grade.

We began to observe that Judy was in Mrs. Hoffman's office in the morning when we walked in the back gym door; in the afternoon at lunch; and when we walked out of the back door in the afternoon. Molly and I even saw Mrs. Hoffman take Judy away from the school in her red Ford convertible.

Everyone seemed to know exactly what was happening but it didn't make any difference. It kept on happening. Molly and I used to giggle endlessly at this relationship we had no name for. We couldn't take our eyes off the evidence that Judy was in love with Mrs. Hoffman and Mrs. Hoffman was flirting with a student. It was tantalizing.

One day we stayed in Mrs. Hoffman's office when we thought she had left in her car with Judy.

Molly opened the closet and found Mrs. Hoffman's favorite leather letter jacket. Molly put it on. She strutted around the desk and admired herself in the small mirror on the wall. I sat in Mrs. Hoffman's special chair she never let anyone sit in. I put my feet up on her desk and twirled in the chair.

At that very moment Mrs. Hoffman returned and stepped into her office. When she saw us she screamed at the top of her lungs. Her carotid artery turned so red it nearly jumped out of her neck.

"What the HELL are you doing in my office? Take that goddamn jacket off now!!! Get out! GET OUT AND DON'T EVER COME BACK!!!"

I put my feet down and ran. Molly tossed the jacket on the desk and ran out the door right behind me. We did not giggle that afternoon.

About a week later, after making up excuses to avoid gym class, I came up with an idea.

I invited Mrs. Hoffman to my home for dinner. I asked my mother and father if she could come. They both agreed. My sister and younger brother were excused from sitting at the table. My older brothers were off to college. Mrs. Hoffman agreed to come.

My father sat at one end and my mother sat at the other. I sat in my usual place -- to the right of my father. Mrs. Hoffman sat between my father and mother on the opposite side of the table.

I have no idea what my mother thought up to serve for dinner. She may have had my grandmother send over her meatloaf and Waldorf salad.

Mrs. Hoffman and my father 'hit it off' discussing schoolboard topics and the idea of girls' basketball teams. Title IX was off in the future.

My mother did her usual silent judging which ran like this: *what does my daughter see in this woman here in my home eating at my dinner table?*

I could hear Mrs. Hoffman's laughter. That is all I remember, that and the fact it went well.

After my dinner invitation which served as an apology I was forgiven for trespassing in her office. And Molly eventually apologized too.

My mind began to drift from the tantalizing doings of Judy and Mrs. Hoffman.

I was more interested in Junior High Co-Ed at the YMCA on Saturday nights. Besides the visible flirtations stopped when Judy went off to senior high school. And Molly and I stopped our giggly shenanigans.

# JUNIOR HIGH CO-ED

WHEN I WAS in seventh and eighth grade all the kids went to the old YMCA gym floor for dances on Saturday nights. It was a big space that could hold many classmates who wanted to dance and socialize. After we danced 'til midnight we all walked over to the greasy Greek diner on Congress Street. They served up French fries and gravy and cheeseburgers to starving hormonal teen-agers. We sat in red booths with small jukeboxes. The rowdiest boys blew straws from girl to girl.

Every week at Co-Ed there were a few older boys from the 8th grade who looked us over.

One boy, S, wore a navy-blue letter sweater every week. He was popular for a few months and both T and I had our eyes on him. T lived close to S and she dated him first. T and I probably didn't have the same taste, but when I saw her dancing with S it compelled me to make a move. I knew T was smart so I thought S must be an okay boy.

I began flirting with S so he would dance with me too. It was out of a seventh-grade stupor of need. What had happened to me since Denny in fifth grade? Nothing. I knew S wasn't really what I wanted as a boyfriend but he was an alarm clock to rouse me out of my funk of ignoring boys. Could I stand another rejection?

Both T and I admired and liked each other as classmates; we would meet up later in the School Street Junior High in tenth grade. T, who shared this boy with me, went on to become the first female student council president in the history of Bradford High. We all voted for her. She later wrote a wonderful piece in my yearbook, the Barker, about "happiness is sharing a boyfriend." It was the kindest way to say we were feeling hormones bouncing all over us and crushes that lasted ten minutes. Those facts had led to our sharing the same boy. And both of us moved on to another boy soon after.

The dear letter sweater boyfriend ended his life in the Bradford hills years later.

# A SPLINTER
# AND A SMILE

IT WAS OUR junior year and we all felt like a Christmas party. Kris and Martha figured out how to have it at the Valley Hunt Club. It was to be a toboggan party with food and dancing afterwards.

I thought it was a great idea. I arrived in the dark. I walked around through the rooms I knew so well because my parents were members and I had been at the Club my whole life. There were snacks set up by Julie the bartender.

"Hi, Mary. What will you have? The usual?"

"Sure."

The usual was a Shirley Temple.

I drank my Shirley Temple and made my way to the restroom to finish putting on warm pants and a jacket so I could brave the cold on the hill. I looked all puffed up and ready to go.

The lights on the hill behind the club were lit up and my classmates were all walking up to the top of the hill behind the horse barn. Everyone settled in together on a toboggan. I joined Dave M and another young man and sat down between them. At the bottom of the hill sat the swimming pool covered in heavy tarp for the winter. The toboggans stopped long before they reached the pool. I could hear the happy laughter of everyone as they sped down the hill.

Dave was a basketball player and a friend so I trusted him to steer. We pushed off and swirled down and down and down to the left and right with total delight in the white snow and stars to guide us.

Then I heard it. WHA WHK WHAM the

toboggan hit a rock! My body went up and then down. The toboggan split into pieces and a large piece of wood entered my back side. I think I heard a few "holy shits" from the boys as they rolled away. Dave helped me up as I was in pain.

I don't remember how I got down to the rest room. Did they carry me? It hurt too much to walk.

I remember my father standing in the girls' rest room. I was on a table and he tried to pry the wood out of my derriere. Nothing moved. It was lodged in deep. E's eyes bulged out as she couldn't believe my father was in the restroom with us. She put her hand to her mouth, feeling empathy for my plight. My father knew by now that we were on the way to the hospital and he was going to be the ambulance.

The next place I could see was the emergency room at the hospital. I was laid on another silver table and put in a johnny. The doctor entered the room. My bum was there bleeding downward on the table. He got his tools and began to pull the wood out of my skin. Then he stitched me up. I knew I was not going to be allowed to go back to the party. I had to go home and rest and come back in ten days for a check-up. My father took me home. I dropped into a deep, deep, sleep as deep as the snow on the hills.

The next morning I was hardly aware of what had happened or where I was until I heard my mother calling to me to get up.

"Mary, time to get up. Our appointment is at 11 a.m."

For a moment I could not recall any appointment. Then it came into my consciousness. We were having our first and only professional family portrait taken by the best photographer in town: Kelly's on Jackson Avenue.

I could barely pull myself out of bed. I dressed slowly cursing the very morning. Then the stitches memory came to me and I touched my bottom. It was sore! But there was the proof that a splinter had ripped my skin.

I put on my rayon blue jumper and white blouse with a bow that tied at the top. I looked presentable for my mother.

We all walked into Kellys' studio. I was given a pillow to sit on once the tobogganing accident was explained. I grimaced a few times during the session. Every five minutes we had to take a break so I could stand up and relieve the weight on my stitches. I tried to smile. The results turned out fine. No one would ever suspect what had happened to me the night before. My mother was pleased with the portrait though it didn't last very long on the bureau in the house.

It was the last portrait done and the last toboggan ride of my life. And my classmates at the Christmas party? They had a good time but years and years later they still remembered the whole incident of the splinter in my bum!

# ZIPPO HIRES NEW DIRECTOR

BRADFORD WAS FAMOUS for the invention of the Zippo lighter. George Blaisdell, a small independent oil producer, invented the lighter in 1932. Though America was in the Depression, Mr. Blaisdell used his ingenuity and created the most famous lighter in the world. It went on to be used by soldiers in World War II and Hollywood made it an icon in movies for seventy-five years.

In the summer before my senior year, a new family came to town. They were the Whitlocks. They had ten children and they were Catholic. Mr. Whitlock was hired by Zippo to head the new golf ball department.

The Zippo board decided to branch out to golf balls now that the lighters were so successful.

The Whitlocks rented a house on Jackson Avenue, two houses down from the Kelly Photography Studio. I didn't see the third son, Michael for a few months because he had been introduced to Zippo's Vice President's family, the Yates. Mrs. Yates was my god-mother and her daughter, Martha, had been with me at my First Holy Communion at St. Bernards. It was summer 1965 and Martha and Michael became a thing.

By fall, when we all entered the new Senior High School, I saw Michael walking down the halls. He was handsome, he had a beauti-ful smile and he was new to our class. Some-how as strangers we found ways to meet each other in the cafeteria and at my locker. I liked the new feelings, but what love could mean was new to me. I also knew he was dating Martha.

But each day he was there in the morning at my locker and after school. We began to wave and smile to each other in the hallways. We were visible to all the other students and suddenly without so much as a conversation with Martha, she was out of the picture. Michael wanted to be with me.

Both Martha and I were nominated for homecoming court. On Homecoming Friday in October, five girls and their escorts road a float at half time at the football game. The girls were voted in by the student body of seniors, juniors, and sophomores numbering 1,200.

It was thrilling to be chosen to represent the student body in the new high school. I found a new blue gown to wear and I asked Michael to be my escort.

Sometime in late September Michael got sick. This was very unfortunate because he was an end on the football team. He was so sick his parents took him to the hospital. He had mononucleosis. He could not be my escort for the biggest night of the year.

I felt so bad for him. He was diagnosed with mononucleosis "the kissing disease" as it was called then. I didn't think we had kissed enough to get him sick. So I wondered what the disease really was. He was gone for a month and a half after football season ended.

I scouted around to find another escort. Lee M, who was a good friend of Michael's offered to escort me.

It was a gorgeous night when the five girls in the court rode around the field and stopped in front of the bleachers. Our queen was crowned by the student council president and everyone clapped. I was not crowned queen nor was Martha or Kris or Toni B; a girl I did not really know was chosen. The cheerleaders jumped and twirled, the band played its tunes. The crowd hooted and clapped. It was a glorious night in the hills of Bradford.

The next day I went to the hospital to visit Michael.

Michael wanted to marry me. It was not something I knew anything about. I thought he should get better before we talked about our future.

My parents seemed to think it was a good idea we marry because they let me sit on the living room couch with him while they went upstairs to bed. We were left alone and trusted.

"Do you want to get married?"

I did not know the answer to Michael's question. It seemed too abstract and bizarre sitting on the couch in my parents' home.

"I think I want to wait," I said.

"Well, don't wait too long."

He took my hand and we kissed again. Whenever we kissed we promised each other we would be together forever.

"I love you," he whispered.

I was silent. In reality neither of us knew what we were talking about. It was young love and cozy there on the couch or lying on the rug at his house on Jackson Avenue.

When his father was caught having an affair

with his secretary, though he had a beautiful charming wife and ten children, the Whitlocks left town. One day the house was filled with love and laughter with Michael and I lying on the rug listening to Johnny Mathis. In a heartbeat they were leaving town after graduation. The family never returned to Bradford. Our relationship did not survive the transition from high school to college.

Michael was happy with me. He wrote a beautiful piece in my yearbook, *The Barker,* describing his feelings of forever and ever.

# FAINTING

WHEN I WOKE up I was in the Bradford Hospital ICU unit. I had fainted on the bathroom floor in the ranch house. It was the morning I was 'in charge' of waking my father and sister. My mother was away at an antique show.

The isolation ward was on the first floor in a separate wing of the hospital. The doctors came in and examined me. I was hooked up to IVs. A nurse stood nearby.

"Hepatitis!" I heard. I had no idea what that word meant.

It was May of my senior year. Suddenly I just knew I was not going to be having any fun the rest of the year. No senior strutting that only happens once in one's life. No freedom to be a senior!

No drives with Michael over to the famous bar, Casey's, across the New York state line. No beers or gin and tonics, or kissing or necking in the car. No more intimate conversations in the dark cavern that was Casey's first floor. No more sneaking off with Michael to the garage attic behind his parents' house to lie in each other's arms. Since we never 'did it' that was not something that was eliminated with my being sick.

It seemed fate had stepped in and taken me to a different place away from my 400 classmates.

The cause of hepatitis, according to the doctors who were quite interested in this case, was shellfish from the Gulf of Mississippi.

They asked me point blank,

"Did you eat shellfish recently?"

"Yes."

In April my mother, father, younger brother and younger sister and I had flown to Biloxi, Mississippi for an insurance convention. My father had successfully sold enough life insurance to qualify for our stay on the Gulf. Though it rained for 4 days we seemed to enjoy ourselves in the swimming pool (in the rain) playing bingo and eating. The meals were mostly fresh shellfish from the Gulf.

The doctor left the room. No one was allowed in the isolation ward including my parents, who along with my younger sister and brother, had to be inoculated. My parents were only allowed to stand in the doorway wearing masks. My grandmother stood outside and waved to me through the big first floor windows.

The nurse looked at me, checked my vitals and said, "You're going to be here for a while."

"How long?"

"A month, maybe six weeks."

*No this can't be. Would I even make it to my graduation?*

I slid down under my sheet and fell asleep.

When I woke I wasn't sure where I was. Then the hills, which were visible from the large windows, anchored me.

It looked like the blue hour as the stars were just beginning to arrive and the sky was a beautiful shade of blue. The nurse came in with saltines and grape juice. This became my night-time ritual: saltines and grape juice after a day of not seeing anyone or talking to anyone except the nurses.

Silence became a new friend. Solitude was there too. After a house full of siblings and parents the quiet was strange at first.

The aqua green curtains in the room were always open for me so that I could look out at the hills. To know my mind was emptying out more and more each day into what I would later understand as contemplation and meditation as an adult was mysterious.

I never had a priest come see me. My father never called for one. My skin and eyes turned yellow. I learned I had AB positive blood which meant I could not donate blood to anyone in my lifetime. But type O, A and B could give blood to me.

I began to let the whole 'pomp and circumstance' idea of walking down the aisle to graduate dissipate. I was thousands of miles away now and no classmate could come see me.

My older brother sent a letter from the Naval Academy at Annapolis. My other older brother wrote me from his first job in Boston at Kemper Insurance. I didn't write back. I had no energy. I didn't talk on the phone, too tired. I never watched television. I was too tired and so I slept and laid there in silence. Silence away from nurses' rounds, visitors, candy stripers, and flowers being delivered. I lay in the hospital bed and saw nothing and no one.

Six weeks went by and I began to heal. I don't

remember walking anywhere to get my diploma though I did graduate. Perhaps someone brought it to me. Activity was still not a part of my life. I was away from so-called reality with my classmates.

What I do remember is my father carrying me up the concrete steps that led to the front door of the ranch house after my discharge. I was too weak to climb. I lost twenty pounds and was very, very thin. He carried me to the side yard to sit in the fresh air. My mother watched speechless. Then she went inside the ranch.

My father brought me a blanket and covered my lap. Though it was a warm day in June, I was cold. He left me to sit alone, then he returned to my mother inside the ranch.

I looked at a bouquet of flowers sitting on the small round table in front of me. The first flowers I could receive outside the isolation ward. *Were they from my siblings? From my parents? From my grandmother? From Michael? Someone welcoming me HOME?*

I kept looking at the pale orange roses. Then I opened the small card.

It was from Miss Mottey, my favorite English teacher. I had missed her talks on *The Return of the Native* while I lay in the hospital bed. Tears filled my eyes when I looked at her fine handwriting and message. Then I noticed a very small box by the roses. I opened it slowly.

There inside was the number one piece of jewelry that all the smart girls wore their senior year. It was a beautiful gold circle pin. Miss Mottey had given it to me because I had graduated and because I had survived hepatitis! I felt the touch of the warm circle pin in my hand.

*I missed my senior year. Missed it. Gone forever,* I thought.

I missed the heartaches and intimate conversations, the triviality and consequences of dating; the teachers and kids seeing each other grow and change all spring, and the life struggle of knowing it was all ending. What would life hold next amidst the break-ups and plans for college and the plans for nothing? I missed the laughter and tears and dashed hopes for anything at all beyond the halls of senior high.

I wasn't sure what would come next. Sitting very alone and weak in the back yard of the ranch house I wasn't even sure I had the strength to go to college in the fall.

Who could know what would come next? I could hardly feel the houses around me or my own frail body.

I took one long, deep, breath and let the fragrance of the pale roses fill me...

There...

in one moment suspended in time....

were the roses...

And then I closed my eyes...

9 781977 252678